T0063031

Also by
Jacqueline van Campen

ARTICLES IN:

<u>Women Overseas: Memoirs of the Canadian Red Cross Corps</u>
Eds. Frances Martin Day, Phyllis Spence, and
Barbara Ladouceur, Ronsdale Press, 1998.

<u>First Drafts: Eyewitness Accounts from Canada's Past</u>
By J.L. Granatstein and Norman Hillmer
Thomas Allen Publishers, 2002.

TEXTBOOKS:

<u>Gens de Chez Nous</u>
By Jacqueline van Campen and Anita Hadley
Irwin Publishing Inc., 1985.

 www.trafford.com
North America & international
toll-free: 844-688-6899 (USA & Canada)
fax: 812 355 4082

Jacqueline van Campen

Medals On My Kitchen Wall

— For my grandchildren —

Nicole

Stuart

Jordyn

Marcos

Laura

Megan

van Campen

And for
Jacqueline Robitaille,
the young woman I was then.

For the pleasure of doing it again.

African Proverb:

*"When an elder dies, it is as if
a whole library has burned down"*

Yup'ik Eskimo Saying:

"Every time an elder, dies a library is lost"

Chapters –

Avant de commencer...

This is not a travel book. It is simply the story of my life between September 1953 and October 1958, at which time I was going around the world working here and there. When I left Québec in 1953 to work for the Red Cross in Korea, I was 25 years old.

In Korea I met M., a social worker from Ontario. We became good friends and decided to meet in Australia after our work with the Red Cross had ended.

When another friend, C., heard of my plans to go and work in Australia, she decided to join me there. I knew C. from Québec; we had hitchhiked to the Maritimes and to New York together. She was also a student at the School of Social Work. She was from Manitoba, and was French Canadian.

The three of us travelled together until M. left for Canada, shortly after we arrived in Sydney. C. stayed with me until we came back home.

M. and C. were marvelous travel companions, through the good and the rough times.

If some of our adventures seem incredible, that is because it was a different world in the 1950s. No better or worse than today I suppose, just different.

My parents, my sisters, and a good friend kept the letters I sent them. I have translated passages from them and have added comments based on my diary and what it tells me!

Some countries, towns, and villages have changed their names since then. My spelling in 1953 was even worse than it is today. I apologize for any mistakes and misspellings you will find.

For my service overseas I received two medals, which I put on the wall in the kitchen to remind me....

Some interesting dates and events
as a background to my story:

Korean War
June 25, 1950–July 27, 1953

Independence and partitioning of
India into India and Pakistan
August 1947

Suez Crisis: Britain invades Egypt
Oct 21, 1951— Four British ships arrive in Port Said
Nov 2, 1951— 6,000 British troops flown into Egypt

Nasser seizes the Suez Canal
July 26, 1956

Apartheid legislated in South Africa
1948

Chapter 1

Québec, Canada

I learned to speak English in Japan! Of course, in my convent school in Québec we had learned a sort of English. In Grade 6 or 7 (I don't remember which), we began with the verbs "to be" and "to 'ave." I don't need to say that there was not an "h" to be heard in the neighbourhood! We progressed from there to other verbs, nouns, and finally sentences—all of this taught by nuns who had never spoken the language themselves. In the middle of my "cours classique" (a humanities curriculum which included Latin, Greek, philosophy, etc. and led to a Bachelor of Arts degree) we were asked to study a short passage from Sir Walter Scott's *The Lady of the Lake* and from Shakespeare's *The Merchant of Venice*. We read the passages aloud in a dialect all our own, but I was well on my way to maturity before I knew what that "pound of flesh" meant.

Later, when I studied with the Ursulines in the upper part of town, I would sometimes meet English-speaking tourists. I did not understand their questions, but being polite and practical I always smiled and pointed to the Basilique or the Château Frontenac—whichever was closer. Later, when I was a tourist myself, I knew to ask directions when I saw that same polite smile from someone else.

But first, let me tell you how it happened that I learned English in Japan. After an adventurous BA and three years of social sciences and social work at Laval University, I went to work as a social worker for a children's aid agency.

In the spring of 1953, I walked into the office of one of my university professors to ask her for some advice. My Master of Social Work thesis was almost finished, but I had to clarify a few points.

I told the professor that I had asked for a six-month leave from my job at the children's aid agency to travel in Europe, which was my life ambition. However, I'd only been working at the agency for six months, and the request was refused. I was very brave even to ask, and that is probably why she shared with me a letter she had just received from the Canadian Red Cross. They needed social workers for the Far East—Japan and Korea. Those who went would work for the Canadian Forces.

I told her that I would write to them. She thought that I was dreaming because:

1. I didn't speak English.
2. There was a war on.
3. I had to finish my thesis.

Well, I couldn't do anything about the war, but surely I could learn to speak English and finish my thesis in the Far East. Since most of the books on social work were from the United States, I was more or less able to read English. I was ready to go anywhere!

I took the letter to our secretary at the children's aid agency (she could write English properly), and asked her to contact the Red Cross for me. They replied very soon after, blissfully unaware that I was not bilingual. They were interested, but wanted to set up an interview with me. As Québec City was very far from Toronto in those days, the Red Cross found a way for it to take place. The director of the Red Cross was coming back from Europe soon on the Empress of Britain and was to land in Québec City. There would be ample time for us to meet before his train left for Toronto—they said!

On the day in question, I went bright and early to the dock at l'Anse au Foulon. The ship was supposed to arrive at 10 a.m. I had anxiously eaten a light breakfast and my anxiety and I were both waiting on the wharf, scanning the horizon like Bluebeard's wife for the white shape of the ship at the point of l'Île d'Orléans.

The director's ship came in at 3 p.m.! By that time I was thirsty and starving. The next problem was finding my interviewer. I asked around and someone suggested that I look for his luggage, as it was unloaded in alphabetical order. I parked myself beside the first letter of his name and waited, wondering how we could misunderstand each other to my benefit. I didn't expect someone from Ontario to speak French. (I was right!)

The passengers disembarked, but there was no sign of my contact. His luggage had arrived and was sitting there. After some worried inquiries, I was told that he was having a drink with the captain. Finally, in the late afternoon, a gentleman appeared who seemed extremely surprised to see me waiting. I explained why I was there and he told me to follow him to the train. We went to his compartment where, maybe to organize his thoughts, he ordered two whiskies. They came straightaway.

I was thirsty, and had never tasted the stuff so I drank the little glass as if it were a soft drink, much to the surprise of my host. He had barely begun to ask questions when the train started to lurch. I got out in a hurry, sure that I had made a mess of the whole thing. It was a strange feeling to find that, upon leaving the train, the platform was coming toward my feet instead of the reverse.

On the bus going home, there were only two passengers, a soldier and myself … both drunk. For me, it was the first time, and almost the last time in my life.

I never expected to hear from the Red Cross again, but a few weeks later, to my great joy, they sent me a letter telling me I had been accepted, and could I return the signed contract. I would leave on the 13th of September for Toronto, Vancouver, and then Tokyo. The details were to follow….

I could not believe it! I was in seventh heaven! I had wanted to go to Europe, and now I was going to the other side of the world. I was so afraid it was a dream that I swore my family to secrecy, got all the necessary shots, arranged transportation for a trunk (a monster which must have taken up all the space for freight), got my uniform, signed here and there, and kept it all a secret until it was time to give up my job.

I liked the people I worked with at the children's aid agency in Lévis and I had a great boss, but I was not prepared to deal with the misery I saw, and the anger directed towards us social workers.

So, on the arranged date, I said farewell to my parents and my sisters. I was in my bright new uniform: gray blouse with Red Cross pin at the neck, a smart tailored serge suit, cotton stockings, regular martial shoes, a purse, gloves, raincoat (smart beige) and a beret with another pin. With everyone giving me advice, I tried again and again to fit that beret on my head. It would not fit properly, so I finally gave up and left with it under my arm.

My plane was a Canadian Pacific (propeller, I think). It was my first plane ride. I don't remember much of it, except for some turbulence between Montréal and Toronto. Ontario seemed such a different world then; it was probably when the plane went over the wall separating these two very different provinces that we experienced all that turbulence!

I had never stayed in a hotel before either, and my first one was the Royal York in Toronto no less! Two girls were to travel with me. B., from Montréal (she was anglophone but spoke French) and K., from Toronto, who spoke only English. Both had problems with their berets too. B. wore hers as a chef bonnet and K. kept hers in her purse. So, our first lesson when we met in the Red Cross offices was on how to properly wear the thing!

The Royal York was the biggest guest hotel in the British Empire. I wrote to my family and told them about the huge room I had to myself on the tenth floor. I ate in style in the dining room, but it was lonely.

On our second day, we went around town and had tea with some ladies in the afternoon. That night we had dinner with some very important Red Cross people at the hotel. We were told in advance that, at a certain moment during the meal, we would be given a small travel notebook. Since these people were our patrons, we were to show our appreciation. K. was a bit more sophisticated, but B. and I were babes from the wood. The meal started with wine ... and carried along with wine. B., who was as unused to drinking as I was, began, just before the dessert, to thank our host for the notebook that we had not yet received! We quickly stopped her, but to this day I wonder what those people thought about sending us lambs to the wolves den!

16 September, 1953   *Vancouver*

We spent only one night in Vancouver. Someone drove us around, and the beauty of the city and the nearby mountains overwhelmed me. Then, on the 17th of September, we boarded The Empress of Mexico, a Canadian Pacific plane bound for Japan.

17th - 19th September, 1953   *The Empress of Mexico*

The Empress of Mexico was a Canadian Pacific ship of the air! But it was not a jet, and I was lucky that we had good weather. It was full of soldiers, a few Canadians, and thirty Americans. Most of them were majors. Cocktails arrived before meals, and the food was good. On the other hand, we had to board and re-board the plane twice in the Aleutian Islands because of mechanical failures. We stopped at an American base in the Aleutian Islands, and at another in Alaska. The plane even had its own stationery. Though a mere detail, it was not called "Empress" for nothing! I wrote home when we had to stop in the Aleutian Islands:

17 September, 1953   *The Empress of Mexico*

I don't know what to do—we are parked with a good fifty men in a mess somewhere on the Islands. The plane needs repairs. I don't know what, but between us, I prefer that they fix it here, rather than making us use those cute life jackets they gave us. I did not see much of Alaska; it was cold but without snow! Here it is even colder. I can't sleep with all these people....

It is strange to see all these soldiers and to wear that uniform with the beret that I hate enough to go to confession about. The plane is comfortable and the flight attendants are beautiful.... I set my watch back every two hours. I am a bit confused....

Before I left Canada, I had not asked too many questions about what the Red Cross was doing in the Far East. I was only puzzled by the fact that they wanted social workers, not nurses.

It was at the request of the Canadian government that the Canadian Red Cross had agreed to send young women to work in recreation facilities for servicemen in Japan and Korea after the armistice. In total, about fifty young women went, twenty of them in the Far East at any one time in the space of four or five years.

Most of the young women recruited were Red Cross personnel and others were social workers and handicraft workers.

I was to find out that my duties as a social worker were limited, if not to say non-existent. We were recreation workers—a cross between Special Service (American) and Women Voluntary Service (English). All this I was to learn as I went along.

Chapter 2

Tokyo, Japan

On the 30th of September, I wrote a long letter home explaining my first week in Japan.

30 September, 1953　　　　　　　　　　　　　　　*Tokyo*

We arrived in Tokyo on Saturday the 19th of September at about 11 a.m. We first flew over Japan at about 9 a.m. It was sunny and I could see the north of the country with its rivers and minuscule fields. In Tokyo, however, we were greeted with torrential rain. My stomach was upset and I had a headache—it was horrible!

Red Cross personnel were there to greet us. We were tired to death, but felt we had to smile and salute. My first contact with the Japanese people was at Customs. The men were very short, always smiling and looking at our pale hair in amazement.

I will try to give you an idea of what I have done since I got here:

19 September

Immediately after we arrived, we had lunch at the Leave Hotel with the Red Cross supervisors here. We are billeted at Ebisu camp, a rest and relaxation centre for Commonwealth military personnel. The Leave Hotel where we lunched is reserved for officers only. My two travelling companions and I went to sleep at 3 p.m., and woke up at 3 a.m. in an apartment with not a crumb to eat.

20 September

Today, I attended Mass at 8:55 a.m. at the camp church. A French-Canadian Red Cross girl who is here in Tokyo took me to the chapel, where there were not even five officers present! Father R., a Dominican and one of my university classmates, celebrated our attendance. After lunch, we went shopping to the Ginza Market (all the shops here are open on Sundays) where everyone must barter with the vendors. I have never seen something so strange, and what merchandise! Kimonos, toy boats with speed gears, lights, sculptures, souvenirs....

At the officers' mess that evening we met two French-Canadian flight attendants who travel from Tokyo to Geneva every month. What fun that would be! We went to bed around 9 p.m., still exhausted.

21 September

Today, I had my first day of work at the Maple Leaf Club from 9 a.m. to 5 p.m. The Maple Leaf Club is a very small club in downtown Tokyo (on the second floor above some shops). It is divided into two parts: a sitting room and a bar. It looks like an English pub. This is where soldiers in Tokyo can congregate (officers are not allowed in), as well as sailors and airmen of the Commonwealth. They come in for drinks; they are all good guys. We see Australians, New Zealanders and sometimes Maoris, who can sing and play the guitar like angels.

Only a few soldiers came in today. I found it quite hard to go and speak to them at the beginning, but I got over it after a while. It was very hard to understand everyone, but they were all very patient. It is wonderful working in town. There is so much to see! The American army has requisitioned hotels, cinemas and restaurants. We can go dancing and see shows. There are some lovely little nightclubs in town as well on narrow streets, seemingly hiding themselves. The jazz is great, lovely soft music and the hostess is ever-present. She is never far, ready to bring drinks, light cigarettes, take plates, or replace you, should you wish to leave!

22 September

B. is leaving for Kure (South Japan). She is heartbroken and so are we.

I worked from 5 p.m. to 10:30 p.m. The Maoris sang

their songs; I like them a lot. In the afternoon, we explored around the camp where we live. It is very beautiful, with a swimming pool and a tennis court.

23 September

Today I worked from 9 a.m. to 3 p.m. I met two Québécois officers from the 22nd Regiment, the best one in the whole of Korea. They fear nothing. They are the regiment nearest to the front. If the war starts again, they will be receiving souvenirs!

In the evening we had cocktails with some French-Canadian officers at the Leave Hotel.

24 September

The aircraft carrier Ocean (British) is in port. I met two very nice officers and went dancing with them at an American club. We really laughed when an Australian soldier told me that he adored me because I was the only Western girl he had seen in six months! He is not the only one to make such declarations. All of us women (seven Canadians, three English, and three Australians) have been told we are the most beautiful women in the world, with the most beautiful eyes! Also, I must explain to everyone where the province of Québec is situated. The New Zealanders, the Australians, and the English all believe we Québécois are part of France!

25 September

A. and I went shopping before going to work. The American army has some stores here that they call PX where we can buy just about everything, almost like a department store. We took the train and everyone stared at us with our long noses and light hair.

The Japanese, when they are tired of waiting, sit down on their heels, and we see entire families (even a woman breast-feeding her child) waiting for the train sitting like that.

We had a terrifying wind last night because of a typhoon.

26 September

I worked from 5 a.m. to 11 a.m., and had dinner with Father R., two officers of the 22nd Regiment, and L. (a Red Cross girl) who is returning to Québec. She will phone you.

Japan has a very special smell, especially when one is behind the trucks that carry the "honey buckets" of the residential "toilettes" – pouah!

So far, I have seen the Imperial Palace, the Diet (the Japanese parliament building), the Imperial Hotel, McArthur Headquarters, and people praying at temples.

It was a very busy night at the Club with some rowdies. Someone broke a window. I was home at 11 p.m.

27 September

I went to Mass at Ebisu, then worked from 1:30 p.m. to 5 p.m. After work, we went to the aircraft carrier Ocean but we were too late to get in. I received some flowers from a French Canadian.

28 September

I worked today from 9 a.m. to 5 p.m. This time, I got three bouquets from some Australians. We have quite a few of them at the Club. There are also some English, and of course, Canadians.

29 September

I went shopping but didn't buy anything. We have been told to wait before spending our money. I have to be patient! Poor me.

It seems as if more and more men are coming to the Club.

30 September

I worked from 1:30 p.m. to 5 p.m. I received an enormous bouquet from a Canadian and a marriage proposal. What to say! Our apartment is like a flower shop!

I am happy to be here even if it is not what I expected. I will get used to it eventually. I work a lot and I don't have time to be homesick.

In reality, my first week in Japan was quite hard. I was tired, and unless I had an interpreter, I missed most of what was said. Then, there was the work. I was not quite prepared to find myself as a sort of hostess, information officer, father confessor, etc. … in the Maple Leaf Club. I never told my parents about my job, as they would have been horrified! According to them (and to me at the time), anyone that drank one or two glasses of beer was a drunkard. Only wine was okay, and a bit of hard liquor for my uncles at Christmastime.

At our Club, the pub was the major attraction, and I was expected to go there and be friendly. Me, in a tavern! All this was made worse when, after a few short weeks, A. (another French Canadian) was posted somewhere else, and I became the only French-speaking Red Cross girl at the Club and at Ebisu.

In the beginning, I was also wondering about my role as a "social worker." It was not quite what I had expected. But it didn't take me long to realize that I loved Tokyo and I liked my job. I also changed my mind about all this drinking. It was not as bad as I had thought at first sight. There was no point in being silly about it—"If you can't fight it, join it" as they say, and so I did. I never drank to get drunk, but enjoyed it for social companionship. Everyone was generous to us and many a potted plant received unwanted drinks that had been given to me. I probably killed a few with my generosity!

I enjoyed talking with the guys who came to the club, and listened to their stories, good, bad and sad. They missed their families and children. I remember a young Australian who was going home to get married, but had changed his mind. Good luck!

The newspapers we had gave them news from home, the music on request was up-to-date, and the beer was very good, so they told me! We were not allowed to drink it at the Club.

18 October, 1953   *Tokyo*

You know that you can't go to a cocktail party without drinking. Yet, that is what I do from week to week. Although I am getting a bit more daring! I may take a sherry or something else, but most of the time I take a Coke. I don't care what people think. We can have milk and cocoa only from the bar. A bit strange perhaps, but this is what I like the best, so here I am (only at the mess, and not at parties), drinking Coke from tall glasses when everyone else sips liquor. I am lucky; everyone finds this cute!

Let us speak about Japan where I can't quite believe I find myself living! At first glance, the town is not beautiful. Most of the houses are about the size of our kitchen at home. On the floor, they have mats and people sit, or rather squat, on them. The Japanese put their shoes on when they go out or if they are serving you in a store. The children are adorable, with their straight, bowl-cut hair and their smiles. Mothers carry their babies on their backs. The people are so polite.

I work irregular hours—9 a.m. to 5 p.m. or 5 p.m. to 11 p.m., without a break. We eat at work. If I work at night, I sleep in the morning and shop or walk around in the afternoon. If I work during the day, I go out at night quite often. I have a free day once a week and I try to go out of town then.

Camp Ebisu, our home, is run by the Australian Army. This base had been an experimental submarine station during the war. It seems strange to think of submarines right in this part of town, but in the camp compound there is a huge reservoir, and great big empty sheds.

I live with N., another Red Cross girl, who is very nice. We live in an apartment with five rooms. We have a Japanese maid who does our washing and ironing (even our stockings!) She polishes our shoes, cleans the flat and magically makes our messes disappear. A very hard life for all of us for sure!

(Eiko-san, our maid, is the daughter of a Buddhist priest and works for us to learn English.)

Our camp has sentinels, of course. Brave soldiers who watch everyone and everything going on. We even have a little changing of the guard everyday. It is rather dull but very army-like. Our building is on a hill to the right of the guard barrier. It is well situated for the interested guard on duty.

Twelve women live in our quarters among about a thousand resident men (admin, etc.) and hundreds of transient troops. As I wrote to my friend: "If the Japanese stare at us, they are not the only ones!" But the only complaint we have, good Canadians that we are, is the tug of war we play with our three English colleagues of the Women Volunteer Service about the heating in our rooms. As it is getting colder and more humid, we close the windows. They open them, and leave them open. We freeze, so we close them, and they open them. To make matters worse, regardless of the weather, the heat will not come on until the 17th of November because of some system of central army control by orders from somewhere. Canadians love their comfort, French and

English alike.

At the moment, it is beginning to get really cold, and it is so very damp. The buildings are made of concrete and the stones are red because of the humidity.

I would like to describe Tokyo to you, but it is difficult. The houses have only one or two floors, only the public buildings have five, or maybe a few more. As a result, from our camp on Ebisu Hill, one can see a multitude of roofs as in an immense village and Mount Fuji on a clear day.

The houses are not painted and that gives a sad look to streets and alleyways. However, now that I am used to it, I am beginning to find it attractive. What strikes me the most is the multitudes of children and school kids that we see wherever we go. There are hundreds and hundreds of them. If you make the mistake of saying "hello," hundreds and hundreds of hands go up and all smile in response.

The traffic in the street is awful. The Japanese drive on the other side of the street from us, like in England, and they always seem to be in a great hurry. It is ten times worse than the worst in Québec. Everyone honks the horn. Terrible!

When I go to work by train, I walk to the station through interesting little streets. I meet storytellers, food vendors, millions of school kids, and pass by lots of little bars. One I noticed in particular had an English advertisement for "cold beer, hot music and medium girls!" Whatever that means!

I expect every base has a string of these bars outside its gates. Because I can't read Japanese characters, all the words on advertisements and notices are as beautiful to me as works of art.

We were invited to a lot of parties, and sometimes were entertained by geishas. I went once to an old-fashioned geisha house with N., a French officer, and a former high-ranking officer of the Japanese Navy. It was in a dark alley, lit only by paper lanterns at the gate. The geishas were older women, and probably very expensive because of their experience and skills. They are companions, not prostitutes, and everything they do to entertain is done effortlessly well, just to please men, of course. I wonder what they made of us clumsy Western women.

In 1953, many Japanese women wore the traditional kimonos to go shopping—not the fancy ones, but a working kind with getas (wooden platform shoes). The platforms were necessary to avoid getting their feet wet as a result of zealous shopkeepers washing down the sidewalk of road dust in front of their stores. We were at a great disadvantage with our leather shoes!

On the subject of women working ... twice I saw old women (in their 50s maybe) carrying their drunk husbands on their backs!

While in Tokyo, I went to lots of temples and kabuki plays. At first, the music in the plays was hilarious: shouting, a bang here and there, the scream of a high-pitched flute or a string instrument. But later I started to like it, especially the koto and the Japanese flute. The plays were acted out exclusively by men. That was puzzling to me, but I liked the costumes, the fights, and especially the sad laments of the heroine (a man of course) when things went wrong.

The plays sometimes lasted for hours, even days, and on platforms around the theatre, families ate, slept and spoke. You could not do that in Québec!

Very often at the entrance to temples, I saw handicapped men dressed in white. These were former soldiers who had been injured in the war and were begging for a living, as well as a number of people sleeping on mats in doorways. The war was not far in the past yet.

Chapter 3

Kobe, Japan

4 December, 1953   *Kobe*

I have been transferred to Kobe. I arrived here after a six-and-a-half hour overnight train journey.

Kobe is in the south of Japan on the shores of the inland sea. The climate is supposed to be milder ... it is very different from Tokyo. Americans are in charge here. At the centre where I am working, I must count people as they come in and go out, write reports, and not work too hard. A. and I are the only two Canadian women here, and I find it very hard. On the other hand, we are only a few miles from Kyoto, Nara and Osaka. These are the most beautiful towns in Japan. Kyoto was the old capital.

15 December, 1953   *Kobe*

Kobe is a seaport, and everyday I see ships like there are in the old part of Québec City. In the background behind our hotel, there are mountains that remind me of the Laurentians. Here, the people dress much more in the old Japanese way. We live in a rich part of town, but there are many poor areas. Even where we are living, people seem to wash themselves and their dishes outside at a tap on the side of the street. The town was bombed during the war and there are a lot of damaged buildings.

This will be my last letter before 1954. Time goes fast. I have been in Japan for three months already. There is talk of sending me to Korea.

30 December, 1953   *Kobe*

Christmas is gone and it was very difficult for me to be in the mood. There was no snow, but mild weather. Christmas is not celebrated here, although this has been starting to change since the end of the war and the occupation. The great holiday in Japan is the 1st of January. Tomorrow night (the 31st) all the bells of the temples will ring and in their houses people will eat special foods and drink *sake*. Children will play special games and dress up in their kimonos. I am anxious to see that.

I went to Kure, the headquarters of the Commonwealth Forces, for three days at Christmas. It was not too exciting.

I stayed in Kobe for the New Year. We took down the Christmas tree at the Club today—just in time—all that was left was a skeleton trunk and the ornaments. And then on the 31st, I had the pleasure of my life. Since my arrival in Kobe, I have been going to Mass every Sunday at the church of St. Therese, which is very near. It is a pretty little church but inside it is terribly cold. I am the only foreigner, with the exception of one other couple (German, I think) to go to Mass there. Everyone stares at me, especially since I first sat on the men's side of the church and I forgot (of course!) to bow to the priest when he began his sermon.

This famous Sunday I was with N., an Australian officer I met in Tokyo. The church was all decorated with fleur-de-lis banners, and then … the choir started to sing! Can you imagine my surprise and great joy when I recognized our Christmas carols from home! And then, all of a sudden there it was, *Il est né le divin enfant* in French! I was crying and N. was also very moved, even if his Japanese is much better than his French. I spoke to the priest who sang. He is from Belgium and helps the two Japanese priests of this parish.

On the 1st of January, I worked all day. You should have seen the people on the streets. The women wore bright kimonos in all colors of the rainbow and the children! How beautiful the girls are in their kimonos and big ribbon bows in their hair. Japan is not a colorful country. Everything is earth-toned. The houses are brown, the temples are brown, the buildings are cement, and the walls are stone and look moldy. But I have not seen Japan in spring or summer yet, when the streets come alive with young girls in kimonos and the beautiful children; then Japan is smiling.

This morning at Mass a mama-san ("san" means "respect") went to communion. She wore a mauve kimono with a baby on her back in a red jacket with a green hood. I thought she was going to drop the baby at any moment.

For the last two days, nobody has been working. Everyone visits one another and they all go to the temples that are like big bazaars. I go between shifts. It is a marvel of colours.

At the moment, the Protestants are leading hymn singing in the lounge. I play the piano for them. When I was in Tokyo it was A. who played for the Protestant service. When she left for Korea they asked me to do it, but because I was leaving Tokyo I couldn't. I told them not to fear—that the new French Canadian would do it for them. Did we all learn to play the piano in Québec at that time? I took it for granted that we did.

The Japanese like everything that is from France. Good for us too!

8 February 1954   *Kobe*

In Kobe there are only two Red Cross girls, A. and me. A. goes home in March, and I am glad to know that I will be leaving here as well on the 17th of March. I will not be sorry. Kobe is very well situated but on the other hand, we are constantly with Americans. It is strange but I feel much more at home with Canadians and people from the Commonwealth. I never realized how different Americans are from us.

English Canadians are very nice and tease me about my accent a lot. When they say that Québec stays in Canada just for the handouts, I tell them that we were in the country before them and because they were fearful and insecure, chickens in fact, they waited for us to get settled down before coming over. We have a wonderful country that we don't appreciate sometimes.

Here I see people sleeping under the bridges, train overpasses, and on the streets. There are people in rags who pick up cigarette butts. The houses in certain parts of town are tiny, with no water, and a fire only if the mama-san can find enough small wood in the fields or on the sidewalks near the building sites.

In January, I went for a week holiday at the Fujiya Hotel near Mount Fuji. I went horseback riding in the mountains and through Japanese villages—it was fantastic. Later when L., a friend of a friend, was visiting from Canada, I went to an island called Awaji. What a trip! I thought I would die. We went in a small fishing boat. We sat in the cabin on the floor with the other passengers, surrounding a big earthenware pot called a hibachi. In it, charcoal was burned to keep us warm. The sea was really rough and my stomach was weak, but I was not sick! Everything smelled fishy on that boat, believe you me! When we landed, we visited a castle that is six hundred years old. Then we came back … the same way. Never again!

I don't have anything to do tonight. It is small games night here at the Army Service Club, which means that I must stay in the office the whole evening, counting the people coming in, changing the music (records) and giving cards and games....

These days we have some very nice guys at the Club. In the beginning of my stay here I was discouraged. I had never seen so many lost-looking young soldiers. But of course, most of these young American soldiers have been drafted. They are very nice and shy. Last week we received a wonderful note from two of these young men:

From W. & J., on behalf of the United States Army in the Far East and the Royal Canadian Army.

To The "Gals" In The Lounge.

Dears Ladies,

Thanks! I want to say this on behalf of all the guys who want to say it, but are the shy type.

Thanks for the swell time we had having music, dancing, eating, reading, writing, and just goofing off in general.

Thanks to all the gals who for some unknown reason stay at the desk and play nursemaid to all the guys, Canadians and Yanks (and rebels), when they could be out making tons of money as movie stars or models.

Thanks to the gals who can have the heart to spend so much time trying to make a bunch of strangers feel a little closer to home.

Thanks for the cookies and cakes that we have wolfed down. Thanks for the coffee that we poured down the hatch.

Thanks too to all the papa-sans who help out around here and to the "Fuji patch" guys and the Canadian Service and Postal Corps too. Even thanks to the MPs (they are like a good woman, I can't get along with 'em, but I guess we couldn't get along without 'em either).

In short "Thanks to everyone for a swell time."

Signed "W." and "J."

* Letter received the 4th of February. Thank you W. and J. You certainly made me feel better!

I love to get books from home. They make me think. To read them in Japan is really strange. The Japanese think so differently from me. What interests me and is at the centre of my world is not the same for them.

Someone is at the desk. I wonder what his problem will be this time?

March, 1954   *Kobe*

A., the terrible, has just left Kobe, and I am very happy. I tried to like her but she was so bossy. N., my roommate from Tokyo, is coming to replace her—a real gift! But then I just learned that I am also leaving. I would love to stay with N. but I am glad I will have the opportunity to see more of Japan.

I will be going to Hiro, which is a little town south of here, near Kure. I will stay there for two months.

Every two weeks, I go in a jeep from Kobe to a hospital in Osaka to visit Canadian soldiers. You should see the town. I feel at times that I am in some part of New York, only the buildings are much lower. The Japanese are very short too, and when I go to Mass on Sunday, I tower over them. (I am only 5 foot 3!) The mama-san walks with small steps in her getas, and papa-san walks as if he was very important. I think that men here must be badly spoiled and think highly of themselves. When a man has a job that has a title, he has many business cards printed, and you see all these men bowing to each other with the greatest reverence.

I can't tell the ages of the Japanese women. They all look to me like little girls. They run and giggle in the hallways of our quarters. What I love about them is their smiles.

Chapter 4

Hiro, Japan

I was lucky to be posted in three different parts of Japan. First Tokyo, then Kobe in the south, and later in a small town called Hiro, south of Kobe. The work was more or less the same, but where we lived was very different.

In Tokyo, I had lived in a Commonwealth camp, and worked at a Canadian Club. Kobe was an American Special Services Centre, our club was downtown and I lived in a hotel. There were only two Canadian girls there and six or seven provosts. We were the only Canadians working in Kobe.

In Hiro, I lived and worked in a Commonwealth centre attached to the headquarters of the Commonwealth Forces in the Far East. Most of the Canadian Red Cross workers were stationed there. I was also posted to Korea later.

What a life! I arrived here on Monday the 22nd, after a six-hour journey by train. I feel as if I am on holiday. To-kyo was a very big town. Kobe was a big town. But here, it is countryside. Instead of living in a hotel (and what a luxury the Koshen hotel was in Kobe) and working in a "soap box" that is on the eighth floor in the middle of town, we live and work in a military camp, surrounded by mountains and rice paddies. It is ideal for spring! Instead of taking almost an hour-long bus ride on ter-rible roads, I have to walk seven minutes under God's beautiful sun to get to work. It is marvelous. Except that it smells a bit because of the fertilizer they use ... you know what I mean!

Read on ... this is my life:

8:30 a.m.	Breakfast in bed
10:30 a.m.	Tea (in bed if I want to)
12:30 p.m.	Lunch
3:00 p.m.	Tea in my room
5:00 p.m.	Tea at the mess
6:00 p.m.	Supper
9:00 p.m.	Tea at the mess
10:00 p.m.	Tea at the mess
11:00 p.m.	Tea at the mess

I have my own maid who does the same things for me as the one I had in Tokyo. Are you jealous? Here I don't have to use my salary for room and board.

I had to pay for everything myself in Kobe and was reimbursed somewhat later. Not only did I have to pay for board, drinks and all services in Kobe, but one day I had to go to an American base for some reason ... I don't remember what ... a yearly physical or a dentist appointment perhaps. Anyway, in the officer's office where I had to wait, everything was labeled "Property of the U.S. Army" and had big price tags! The chairs were labeled, the desk, the in-out trays, lamp, typewriter ... to deter black market thieves, or just to show where their taxes went ... I don't know which!

Now, with money in my pocket, I will be able to shop for you. Another great thing about Hiro is that I work with Australians and New Zealanders. They are so nice. I am very happy right now. It was a good thing I was in Kobe in the winter though. We were well heated by the Americans, while the people working for the Commonwealth froze all winter.

I have to send you a few things but you can see I am very busy, working, eating, resting and tea drinking!

1 April, 1954   *Hiro*

It is marvelous to be back with Canadians and to be with so many of our Red Cross group. As I said before, Hiro is the headquarters of the Commonwealth in the Far East. Our job is to keep the guys busy and this is where I show my real lack of skills! I was born with hundreds of feet (good for travelling) but no hands. I have no talent for anything resembling crafts. Some of the members of our group are specialists and I try to help them somewhat.

Counselling is out of the question. Only the supervisors are allowed to do it, and even then, the army has its own counsellors.

I go to all the dances and bingo. (My 33, pronounced "tirty-tree," is a big hit.)

In Kobe, I was under-employed. Here in Hiro, I am unemployed but I love the place. It is truly Japan, with the farmers, the rice fields, the rivers and the villages. The mountains surrounding us are covered with cultivated terraces. All is green now and we can see some funeral stones. When I feel brave enough I will climb some of the hills and take photos.

This afternoon I went shopping with my girl-san—she looks after me like a mother. If you could only see Chekiko bargaining, it is a sight! Nobody can take advantage of her! Coming back, I saw some oyster fishermen in bare feet in the mud up to their knees with big cone-shaped hats to protect themselves from the sun. There were three mama-sans, one with a baby on her back, untangling the nets.

I must stop. There are three guys in the lounge. I must go and speak to them—thank God I love to talk!

Later that day

If you could see me in my shorts, in the sun! What a good life this is. Yesterday it was dance night, like all Fridays, and I met some guys who were with us in Tokyo. One was so happy to see me that I thought he would project me over the building. What is great is that we see each other often enough to become friends but not often enough to start arguing. That way, we have good memories of each other.

In the middle of the month in Japan, it is the Boys' Festival. We are beginning to see the pennants that people fly over their houses. It is also blossom time. In a week it will be even better. It gives colour to the towns that are so neutral and it makes the villages which are so beautiful even more so.

I can find my way in English now. It is funny to be able to hear the different accents.

5 April, 1954   *Kure*

Kure is about 20 miles from Hiroshima, where the Americans dropped the first atomic bomb. I'd love to go around some more but the Canadian government treats us like priceless little chickens!

Before leaving Kure in May of 1954, I went for a vacation of seven days to the sacred island of Meyajima, where the Commonwealth troops had a centre. It was so wonderful to have a vacation.

7 May, 1954   *Meyajima*

I took the opportunity while I was on the island to consult the gods about my future. No wedding in sight but later it will happen suddenly! He will come from the East! They also told me that I will be sick for a while and the full moon is the best time for me to make decisions. What a lark! To find out all that I had to go to a temple.

I rang a bell and a monk dressed in white and yellow appeared and gave me a piece of paper with some characters after I had taken a number from a bunch of sticks. If my fortune was not good I could have chewed it and spit the paper on the wooden statue of the god (a horrible looking one).

The truth is that I went to this island not to find my fortune, but to finish my thesis and though I did work at it a bit, I hope to finish it in Korea.

I have to say a few words about that famous thesis. Before leaving Québec, I had put it in my monster of a trunk. It arrived in Tokyo two months later, but by then I had such a busy time at work, without mentioning a great social life, that I could not get to work on it. I was riddled by guilt and it became to me what a ball and chain is to a prisoner. I never finished it.

Meyajima (where I finally gave up on my thesis) is a sacred island where nobody can die or be born. During the last war, it was there that the kamikaze pilots spent their last few days. It must have been impressive then. They spent a lot of time going to the temple to pray to their gods. For each pilot that died there is a stone lantern. At night, all light up—it is an eerie sight.

It is a strange island. During the day it is full of tourists and schoolchildren. After the last ferry at night, there is nobody except the clients of the different Japanese hotels (ryokans) who go around in their yukatas (cotton kimonos provided by the hotels), strolling and shopping. Many have had too much sake!

Also on holiday with me was an English sergeant, J.,

whom I had known in Hiro. We took the last ferry trip to the mainland and back one evening. He played his harmonica. It was great fun. The passengers thought that we were crazy. The next day, we went to a dance in a dance hall full of Japanese people. I was a sensation (excuse me for bragging!) It was lots of fun also.

J. had a surprise for me. At home, I had taken for granted that England was one hundred percent Protestant, but my friend came from a Catholic family that had never changed with Henry the Eighth. I thought the same applied to Holland. I had a lot to learn—not only about religion!

I also had a surprise for J. To his great shock, I was wearing jeans. I normally only wore them in our quarters on the bases or on holiday. They were not in the least bit ladylike! I knew that, but I was on vacation after all!

Japan is a fascinating country. I loved it. My only regret is that I did not get the time I needed to get to know the Japanese themselves. Because I worked irregular shifts, it was hard to make plans or establish any sort of routine. We were not encouraged to mingle ... so to speak. In Kobe, a young Japanese journalist who called me Jacquie was reprimanded by an American MP, much to my chagrin, for having referred to me so familiarly. Our own MP (in Kobe) couldn't do anything but suggest that I not be so friendly with the locals while working there!

Because we were part of an occupation army, the U.S. had requisitioned clubs, hotels, restaurants and cinemas for their own troops, as I have said before. We were welcome to them and sometimes used them, as, for example, the hotel I stayed in during my time in Kobe. This way it was also quite easy and reasonable to travel and stay in most places in the country.

Letters to my family and to my friends do not quite tell the whole story of Kobe. In Tokyo, I was very happy. We had so much to do. Japan was a treasure of marvelous things to see. I could go anywhere by myself, explore and shop. Our quarters were comfortable. I didn't speak enough English at the beginning to feel discrimination and I don't think there was any. Maybe just slight puzzlement at my ways. I was also amazed at how I looked at things compared to my English colleagues. We all had busy social lives.

Kure was a different "pair of sleeves" as the French expression suggests! There were only two of us, a senior woman and myself. That senior woman did not have a good reputation for co-operation and good working relations with other Red Cross girls, as I later found out. I think I was sent because I was easygoing (that changed a bit as my English skills improved!)

She was very controlling, and built a shell around me. After the frantic pace of my social life in Tokyo, I found myself limited to going out with only her and our American Service Corps boss at the centre who, if it is possible, was even more of a control addict. Both of them were older than I (in their 40s). They meant well and wanted, no doubt, to protect my virtue. But that was something I was quite capable of doing, thank you, and in both languages!

Kobe did, however, have some advantages. It was close to a great many beautiful spots and lovely towns in Japan. I tried to go to them all—most of the time on my own—but still I was very lonely and it was a joy to meet the few Canadians I saw at work. Americans were different. Some officers had their families with them I think. As for the GIs, they were shy or not interested. Most of our activities were organized by the chaplain and his wife. They included dances, bingo, films and shows. I saw Louis Armstrong, but missed the Ink Spots at our hotel—I didn't have enough money to go! I served coffee and cake at the activities, and counted how many people came in, played records and tried to chat with a few in the lounge. I noted in my diary that often Japanese girls refused to dance with black GIs—if I could, I would dance as often as possible with them.

Chapter 5

25th Canadian Brigade, Korea

7 May, 1954   *Korea*

Well, here I am in Korea. I came by plane. It took three hours from Iwakuni, Japan. We stopped for fifteen minutes in Pusan before landing in Seoul. Being the only woman on board, I was invited to see our plane landing from the cockpit! The ground comes to you faster than you can imagine!

After that, it was two and a half hours by Jeep to the 25th Canadian Brigade, where I am now.

What a country! I am afraid that I won't see much of it. We are about a mile from the Chinese, the brave, and me! So far I have the impression that I am camping— the only difference is that women are scarce! I live in a Quonset hut, a sort of metal shed with a half circle roof, with four other Red Cross girls. It is not bad if you think that everyone else here lives in a tent. It gives me a taste for what it must be like to live in an army camp in times of war.

If you could see me right now, you wouldn't know that I am in Korea. I am in the living room of our Quonset hut where there is a carpet, tables, armchairs, lamps, a radio … it could be anywhere in the world. Except for the ceiling, which is round like an igloo, the mouse that just passed between my feet, and the lights that flicker because of the generator. And there is always someone in the distance who is practicing with his machine gun.

I have so much to tell, even after only three days here, that I don't know where to begin. To see all these tents around, mostly in clusters here and there, makes me think that I am back with the Girl Guides. Only there are the tanks, the checkpoints, the sentinels, the trucks … and all these men. There are about five thousand of them just around here. It does not look as if there are so many as they are spread all over the place, but on Sunday night they came to the movies at the cinema in Maple Leaf Park and there were a lot of them! The guys come in truckloads of about fifty to go to the cinema or to the library at the centre where I work with three of the other girls. It gives me the impression of working in a general store in a remote village where there is nothing else.

Last Sunday, I passed by the line-up at the cinema on my way to work after having supper in the mess tent. All the men were whistling, laughing and shouting greetings (I hope!) It was so embarrassing I wanted to go underground.

But the guys who come to the centre are very nice. They talk about home and show us photos as if we were their big sisters. They are bored and homesick—they are so happy to get letters. On my first working day here I met the brigadier. He gave us a lift back home. He was happy to have met the only French-Canadian girl here (me!) Everyone was saluting us … it made us feel important!

I eat in a brown tent. The food is good and there is plenty of it. The cook and the waiters are French Canadians. As a consequence, I get, in a way of speaking, special service … I can ask for anything!

When I first went to the Club there was a soldier who was speaking French with another guy. Of course, I spoke to them—but heavens, the next day there were at least twenty of them wanting to talk. I can hear the machine guns as I write….

I wrote to M. that I was about one mile from the front. It is not true. I am nine miles south of the demilitarized zone, which is north of the 38th parallel. The river Imjin is at the bottom of the hill where our living quarters are. I go over a bridge called "Pintail" (which means nothing to me) to get to it. The fields are mined around here and the soldiers tell us, "Here we fought, here this happened, here that happened." I asked what would happen if the war starts again. They reassured me by saying that if it did, we would be the first to be evacuated. So don't worry, if there is danger you will find me coming home: the brave Jacqueline who went to Korea after the war!

I received your parcel with maple sugar and the chocolate Easter bunny the day before Easter! I shared it with my friends. Since we had nothing else it made Easter for us.

It is strange in this place. I go to the movies and I am the only woman! I can't count the bits of paper I get, even flying chocolates from admirers! When we go on the road there are almost accidents as the men turn to salute us! They wave as long as we are around. I said the other day that I would love a pie. One arrived last night … a real fancy one from the cook of the Guards Regiment!

11 May, 1954   Korea

Yesterday we tried to organize some square dances. The guys had fun and us girls (there are only five of us) worked hard and were flying in the air.

But this is not all we do! At the Brigade Headquarters (Maple Leaf Park) we run a library, we play cards (I always win!), we organize and run some clubs and we just chat! Each of us speaks on "Radio Maple Leaf." I always say something in French. It is interesting to hear the guys' comments; I have the beginnings of a fan club!

I have asked for an extension to my tour of duty in Japan. I will be staying just past September of this year. So I will be back home in December 1954, instead of September 1954 as originally planned.

I will go back to Japan after my time here in Korea—I don't intend to buy too many souvenirs as I am saving to go to Europe!

Today there have been maneuvers on the hills around here—they are going on even at night. Our hut is on one of the hills where the Forces' personnel come for retreats. The camp chapel is also on our hill and the two chaplains, one Catholic and one Protestant, also live there. Of course I play the little organ for both services! The Protestant chaplain likes music of a sort—he has bagpipes and seems to practice for hours! It is torture for me.

12 June, 1954   *Korea*

I have already described the kind of hut I live in. It is not bad and my colleagues are okay. But since we are under the protection of the army, life is somewhat difficult. I have a curfew of 11:30 p.m. We can't go anywhere except in pairs, and our movements are restricted.

We are in the rainy season at the moment. Every three days the weather is nice, the rest of the time it buckets rain.

I went for a ride in the Jeep today. It was not very comfortable. We go fifteen to twenty miles per hour, and the dust!

We have our own driver and a Jeep. Going out of the camp is out of the question, but we have been on a trip to a nearby English officer mess and other nearby messes.

In the past, we have gone on short trips, to the 38th parallel marker, for example.

12 July, 1954   *Korea*

I am sitting in front of our hut, behind the screen (so as not to distract the good guys on retreat!) In front of me there are hills and valleys. It is 6:30 p.m. It was nice today, and we used the good weather to make a trip from the front lines to a field hospital to see one of our colleagues who is leaving for Japan. We "ate" a lot of dust on the way, but we had a lot of fun too.

On our return, we went to a nearby village to take some photos. These villages are out of bounds so we must take our photos from the jeep. We could see young girls with cooking pots on their heads, and young boys with wooden A-frames on their back. They carried loads that were twice as high as they were.

I like Korea. It is a nice country, with its hills, rivers and valleys. Houses are made of dry mud on wooden trellis and the roofs are thatched. They are generally in an "L" shape. Koreans dress in white, in perpetual mourning for their ancestors.

I don't know if you have any idea about the way rice is cultivated. They must plant the seedlings one by one with their feet in the mud. Their white clothes are not the most practical for that type of work.

I haven't yet found the man of my dreams. Having too many men around, and not having enough is the same thing.

23 July, 1954   *Korea*

It has been raining here for the last fifteen days. The water in the Imjin River below our hut has risen twenty feet in four days. I was told it can get to a maximum of forty feet before it really floods. We are always wet. We are lucky to live in our Quonset hut. It is more comfortable than our tent.

Our hut was comfortable, but it had no running water so we had to go outside in all sorts of weather to an outhouse. As for washing, we had to make do with a basin of hot water.

Two Korean girls shared our hut and cleaned, washed (in the creek with a stone) and brought water. Since we had power, we were able to heat it up.

Showers were special, and could be had only at the Maple Leaf Park. I noted the first time I had one. I went in our jeep with another girl. We had to barricade ourselves into an old brown tent that was full of holes! It must have been borrowed from a M*A*S*H unit nearby!

The only things I can buy here are toothpaste, English chocolate, and shoe polish! Last week someone got into the office where I work and stole three of our purses. I lost a lipstick and one dollar. Lucky me. The two other girls lost fifty dollars, twenty dollars, a pair of glasses and a lighter.

There is a medical doctor here with the Canadian Guards who hardly speaks English. When he does his accent is terrible—like mine. My Red Cross friends find it extremely funny when we venture to speak English to each other. We are good friends, these girls and me.

I play chess like a pro now. We have set up a camera club, had an amateur night, bingo, and a dance (with seven girls, three of whom we borrowed from the medical hospital unit further south) and two hundred guys. Have you tried dancing with men in army boots! It was martial shoes for the seven of us girls. Ouch!

I work from 10 a.m. to 4 p.m. or 4 p.m. to 9:30 p.m. Not much, but at least it is always at the same place.

I am glad you liked the wallet I sent you. Our choice is limited here, unless you would like some toothpaste!

It is still raining and the roads are "red" which means you stay put!

7 August, 1954 Korea

I thought I would stay in Korea until September, but there has been a change of plans and I leave on the 11th of August for Tokyo. I am sorry to go, but look forward to going back to Japan. I am only afraid that I will be tempted to spend all my money!

Looking back, I wonder how we all lived in peace together under the same roof ... and worked together as well. How do the nuns do it! It should have been easy, as there were only a handful of us at a time in the small Quonset hut. The problem (as I see it now) was that most of the supervisors at our postings were older social workers with a lot of experience dealing with clients, but little knowledge of how to handle young women.

A couple of the girls had steady boyfriends, but for the rest of us, there was little to do in the evenings. We had only the kitchen and a small sitting room, so most nights it was bed for us, or the kitchen. A few of our supervisors had no sense of humor whatsoever, though we had some good ones as well, of course.

Thank God M. and B. came during my last month in Korea. We laughed and had a good time. It was then that M. and I first had thoughts of going to Australia after our tour of duty.

Chapter 6

Tokyo, Japan

18 September, 1954   *Tokyo*

Last year I left Vancouver on the 17th of September and arrived in Tokyo on the 19th. Now, one year later, I am back where I started in Tokyo (losing a day in the process). Since then, things have changed here at the Maple Leaf Club. The war is a thing of the past. The soldiers now have no experience of it. They certainly drink less. I have just learned that two-thirds of the Canadian Brigade will be home before Christmas. I don't know what it will mean for us. Lucky me, I have now been posted everywhere. I am one of the few, if not the only one, to have worked in all the Red Cross centres in the Far East.

M., my good Red Cross friend, is leaving for Australia on the 20th. She is taking a passenger ship and will stop in Hong Kong and possibly Formosa. If I leave in December as planned, I will try to take the same ship. I will go to meet M. in Melbourne or Sydney. In March, C., from Canada, will come to meet me in Australia. In May ... maybe Europe.

Poor you. You must think that I am crazy. I am very selfish. Instead of coming back, I leave you all alone at home. The bright side is that when I return, it should be for a long while....

The Club is now busy, so I must go.

Later that day

Yesterday I went to a ball and the night before to a dance. I had a nice dress made. It was three-quarter length in blue taffeta with an organza silk shawl on top. The silk has silver threads. It cost me ten dollars for all the material and ten dollars to have it made. It was not expensive for something like that.

I don't write such a coherent letter today. When you go to bed at 4 a.m. and 2 a.m....

The other day, we were guests at the sergeant's mess here in Ebisu. They offered me a drink. I took a Collins, then they gave me three more! One was left on the table, the other behind my chair and I drank the third one. The moral of the story is that one Collins is enough!

Sept/Oct 1954   *Tokyo*

There was a festival at the Meiji Temple today (which is named for the emperor of the same name). There were archery contests with archers dressed in ancient Japanese costumes. We saw some dancing geishas but, my gosh, what a crowd.

In Japan, there are lucky days: Monday, Wednesday and Saturday. This is when one gets married and presents babies to the gods. Shintoism is the predominant religion here.

2 October, 1954   Tokyo

Great news … I will be going to Australia in December. I have already reserved my passage on a ship. My cabin number is 57D.

I have been back in Tokyo since the beginning of August. The town is the same. For me it is almost like coming home. I met an Irish captain who wanted to marry me because I am such a nice Catholic girl!

I am going out with D., a captain from New Zealand. We go to concerts and operas. It is nothing serious, just good friends. It is strange for me to go out with people from all these different countries. We go to the most expensive and chic places in town. I will need a castle when I come back home! However, starting in December I will live on water and biscuits until I find work in Australia. My English is not giving me problems anymore. I am now bilingual.

5 October, 1954   Tokyo

Right now it is 2:30 p.m. and I am sitting in the sun, which is very warm. I am listening to Tchaikovsky's overture *Romeo and Juliet*. What a life! Tomorrow I am on leave and head for Choshi by the ocean.

I will stay in a ryokan (a strictly traditional Japanese hotel) on the beach with nothing to do for five days ... it is my last holiday before leaving Japan.

M. has already gone to Australia. I am waiting to hear from her. Her trip on the ship will take a month. She will stay a week in Hong Kong. I am travelling with the same shipping company. My ship is called the Changsha.

Your Christmas gifts this year will not be great, as I have to save my money.

I know some people in Australia that will help me and now that I can type, I can do all kinds of work.

I had bought a typewriter for my father, along with a "teach-yourself-to-type" book. At the ryokan, I practised up so I would have an employable skill when I reached Australia!

To reassure you, here is the state of my fortune. When I leave Tokyo on the 1st of December, I will have:
$600 in the bank
$500 in Victory Bonds
$350 owed to me from Kobe (where I paid for every-thing, remember?)

It comes to a grand total of $1450. I have to pay $268 for my passage. When you realize that I have earned $170 a month, plus two extra months of pay, it is not that bad.

C. arrives in Sydney on the 9th of March.

C. was a classmate from Laval University who had hitchhiked

with me at home. When I told her I was going to Australia, she decided to meet me there. We were good travelling companions, and were to stay together for the duration of our journey.

8 October, 1954   Choshi

I am on holiday here for five days. Every fourth month we have a week's leave. The first time I went to Kyoto, the second time to Meyajima and this last one I will spend here in Choshi, a fishermen's village. It is beautiful. In our ryokan we sleep on the floor and live in kimonos and our bare feet. Since we are on the sea we eat lots of fish, lobsters, crabs, fish soup, etc. Our room is on the second and highest floor. Except in the business section of Tokyo, nothing is higher. At the moment, I am sitting like an Indian wise woman (minus the charms!) looking out at the sea and its waves crashing on the rocks below.

It makes a thunderous noise and when I go to sleep at night on the tatami, I think that I am on the bridge of a ship. I can see a dozen fishermen's boats returning to the village next to us. There is a lighthouse nearby and at night it reminds me of the one in the Saint-Laurent, except that the sea is calm around l'Île d'Orléans, and it is not calm here.

Three weeks ago I went to swim, or rather, play, in the surf at Kamakura. The waves were seven to eight feet high. I didn't go very far, as you know that I really can't swim.

For these five days here I have been reading, writing, walking around, and eating! I go to bed very early, at

6:30 p.m.! Just before that I go down to the "honourable bath." We have to wash first and rinse before we go into the hot bathtub for a little dip. An older papa-san wanted to help and rub my back! I got out of there red like a lobster. The water is so hot, but I feel fresh and rested.

If I want, I can share a bath with the other ladies at the inn because, according to Japanese custom, baths are social places. You don't notice (I would!) who shares it with you—man or woman. You can gossip while you bathe!

10 October, 1954   Choshi

This morning I went to Mass in the next town. The priest is an Australian from Melbourne. We chatted a bit. He is alone, there are very few Catholics here, but he is happy. He is young and looks like an athlete. He will probably spend his life among these people who are probably the hardest in the world to convert.

It is interesting to go to a Japanese church. First you leave your shoes outside, then you pray in Latin, just like you do at home.

Yesterday we went to another fishermen's village. It had narrow streets and wooden boats. We had a little trail of children who followed us wherever we went like the parade of Saint John the Baptist. Their families were just as curious and amazed to see that incredible sight—two Western girls, one with yellow hair ... how much more popular can you be!

19 October, 1954   *Tokyo*

At the moment, there is an Australian marching band visiting Ebisu. They march in their big hats that look somewhat like the Boy Scouts. They sound good. Three cheers for the Australians!

Tonight we have a dance as we always do on Wednesdays. The "Irish Fusiliers" band will play. It will be great. I have danced with so many people with so many different styles that I can claim to be an expert. I know how to dance like the English, the French, the Canadians, even the Dutch!

16 November, 1954   *Tokyo*

My ship to Australia is really a freighter that takes a few passengers as well. Right now, there is a dock strike in Australia and my ship will be late. I will leave in the middle of December. I will be one of seventy passengers.

Later that day

As of 9 p.m., we have had another change of plans. Now, my ship will not be here before January.

4 December, 1954   *Tokyo*

I miss listening to French songs. I will write down which English ones are in great demand at the Maple Leaf Club:

Little things mean a lot
Cross over the bridge
Wanted
I get so lonely
Make love to me

All six of us girls decorated the Club yesterday and whoever else was there helped. There were some Kiwis (New Zealanders), Aussies, Canadians and some very nice English boys. There was also a tall (6'2") Dutch guy who had come especially to see Jacqueline with her so very cute accent.

He is very good looking, but as my work requires that I chat with everyone and smile, he was not too happy when he left. Poor me, another possible one who could be a candidate for marriage if I had tried harder! I say "another one" because I get at least a couple of offers (not serious), about twice a week. They have the "coup de foudre." Once I return home, if nobody tells me that I am great and cute, I will have to find someone who will volunteer to do it!

14 December, 1954   Tokyo

It seems settled. I leave on the 28th of December from Kobe. On Sunday, I go to Kure, then to Kobe. In a week, I begin the trip of the year!

It is about time for me to leave. I dream of ships and kangaroos! When I walk around Tokyo, I feel that it is a ghost town, but I leave Japan happy. I have seen what I wanted to see. I would have like to have shopped more, but it is better to see Australia than to spend my money on brocade and ivory.

It doesn't look like Christmas here in Tokyo. It is warm, more so than last year, according to my memory.

Without snow it is difficult to get into the festive mood. For Christmas, I go back to Kure, where I was bored to tears last year.

I am so surprised that no one from Laval University has come to work here. What is everyone doing? When I decided to come here, I felt that all of the province would follow.

Chapter 7

MV Changsha
China Navigation Co.

1 January, 1955   *MV Changsha*

Happy New Year! I am finally aboard. Let's hope we leave soon. I only wish that there were some young people among the passengers besides N. (an Australian officer and friend from Tokyo) and me! If I had to put a "book title" to our sea trip I would call it *Two Children with a Multitude of Grandparents*!

After lots of adventures in our relationship, N. and I find ourselves on the same ship to Australia! I had the shock of my life to find him here. Did he know I would be going by ship? Really, he is quite sweet. Remember him from last New Year in Kobe?

Australians on board are listening to the races today, but me? I am reading a mystery novel. I wish you could join me … we could open a bottle of wine and sing Christmas carols….

Which just now gave me an idea. I opened the piano. A little girl from Scotland appeared out of nowhere, and sang the carols I played for her. She rolls her r's when she speaks, like all Scottish people. She behaved like a lady!

The ship has not left yet, so now I will have tea. There is a party on board tonight and I am going.

14 January, 1955   *MV Changsha*

It is the middle of January and I am dying from the heat. We finally left Kobe on the 2nd and we arrived in Hong Kong on the 7th, after five days of very rough sea. We caught the tail end of a typhoon. My cabin is the cheapest. I think it is right beside the propeller or at least very near. Here I thought that I had inherited good sea legs from my river pilot ancestors! I was very seasick, which was not a pleasant experience.

In Hong Kong, I had four marvelous days. I think that I saw everything. An officer from one of the Canadian ships in port took me sightseeing—to restaurants, night-clubs and to the Peak, which overlooks the harbour side of the island. I was spoiled.

After Hong Kong, we had again two days of extreme-ly bad sea.

From Kobe to Hong Kong, I was alone in a cabin meant for four people. Now I have three Russian ladies with me. They come from China where they had a rough time. And that, after leaving Russia after the revolution. They have interesting stories to tell.

The last three days have been great. At 7 a.m., I swim in the canvas pool on the upper deck. Breakfast is at 8:30 a.m. At 9 a.m. I go to the deck where I read for a while. I eat at 1 p.m., then I go back on deck to read or sleep. Tea is at 4 p.m. Yesterday I got my first tropical sunburn.

On our way to Hong Kong, I saw Formosa (Taiwan) in the distance. Later, we also passed near Manila. Everyday we see many islands and this morning we crossed the Equator. There was no ceremony, as the passengers are too old! I wish you could see the flying fish, dolphins, sharks, and all these islands.

I still have a week to go on this luxury cruise! We will stay five days in Brisbane. I should see the Southern Cross tonight or tomorrow.

20 January, 1955   *MV Changsha*

We just passed a small island. I looked at it with a pair of binoculars. It looks like a coconut tree plantation with little huts and their thatched roofs on the beach. I have not seen snow since leaving home with the exception of Mount Fuji, and then, it was only from a distance. I miss it.

It is 11 a.m. They just brought us some fruit juices. A week ago it was "beef tea!"

The only trouble with this ship is that I am the only young woman aboard. We have old people, a few couples with children, and three Japanese women with their Australian husbands. We have twelve officers, eight of whom are of my age group. I am having a great time but would not mind another girl for company.

I am in Australia. I can't believe it. What a strange place it is. It is hot, and bananas, dates and lemons grow everywhere. I've been to Mass with an Irish officer from the ship. At the church, the men were in shirt sleeves, and the women wore three-quarter length sleeves on their dresses and huge straw hats. It seemed old-fashioned to me.

Today I went to a beach with big surf and miles of white sand and blue sea. It was out of this world!

So far, Australia seems to be a marvelous country—like Canada, but in a very different way. In town, each store has a roof over the street with pillars. It is like a Western film set. The men wear felt hats with large brims.

The houses are built on piles to protect them against ants. They have no basements, but plenty of room under the houses for all sorts of things. Everyone lives in bungalows. They have lots of room in front for a garden, as well as in the back. The town is spread out too, in order to have bathroom facilities for all. Except for the centre of town, every house has a little outhouse shed in the back garden as well as a water tank on the right side.

Yesterday, I went swimming at a centre called The Oasis. Also, yesterday, on our way to church, a tram conductor stopped to show us where the church was. We took a taxi back in the afternoon and our driver swore vehemently at the traffic. They drive on the wrong side of the road here.

Chapter 8

Melbourne, Australia

I am really here in Melbourne! I arrived last Friday. M. met me at the train station (because the states had different gauges for their train tracks, we had to transfer at the border of the states of Queensland and New South Wales). She shares a room in town with my former Red Cross supervisor in Japan. I slept, washed up, and had a meal there. Then the W. family (the parents of an Australian Red Cross girl I met in Japan) came to get me. I could not refuse to go with them, they are so generous—I will stay at their house until the 8th of February.

Tomorrow I start looking for a job, probably at a playground. They are open all year around here.

My hosts, the W. family, are the nicest people in the world. They have a car, and last weekend (Australia

Day) we went to Blackwood, a village in the country, for three marvelous days. I saw kookaburras, gum trees (eucalyptus) and the real Australian bush. I also saw some children on horseback. We lived in a real country house and our hostess never stopped baking ... paradise. We didn't want to go back to Sydney. We sang, we ate, and M. and I played duets on a piano made in Canada.

C. is coming a bit later now. She will arrive at the end of March.

2 February, 1955   *Melbourne*

Australia is a very nice country. They dress a bit old-fashioned and many look like ranchers. The Australians are very friendly and will speak to you at any time. They drink tea constantly, and are very sensitive about what we think of their country. They are certainly more English than Canadian. I like them a lot.

6 February, 1955   *Melbourne*

Life is really strange! I found a job at a playground and was due to start tomorrow but....

On Sunday I went to Mass at St. Patrick, the Melbourne cathedral. During the sermon, the priest made a desperate appeal for schoolteachers. Egged on by M., who came to Mass to keep me company, I went to offer my help. I must have been crazy! To my great surprise and astonishment I got a job as a teacher. Me, a teacher! I have forgotten how to count in French, let alone in English!

It seems that there is a great shortage of Catholic teachers in Australia; I almost cried during the priest's appeal because it was so desperate. I started this morning.
I don't have a class yet; at the moment I am helping the
other teachers. The priest, a Marist Father, is very nice.
I am still living with the W. family. It is a home away
from home.

I can't adequately describe what happened just prior to the
start of the school year at the Sunshine Catholic School of St.
Peter Chanel in Deer Park better than Father G.! This is what he
wrote in the March 1955 issue of the parish bulletin:

Parish Bulletin: "Ave Maria"

Sunday, 6th

Now, on Saturday afternoon, where could I find
two teachers for school on Monday. By the provi-
dence of God I was due to preach at the Cathedral
at all of the Masses on the following day to make
an appeal for funds to help rebuild our burnt-out
church. Gathering my bucket of blood and bottle of
tears, I went forth and begged for help.

Said first Mass at Cathedral and preached at all
others. Felt desperate. Called for help. Amazing
generosity of the people. Jacqueline Robitaille—a
French Canadian on her way around the world—offered to come and help with the younger children
until she leaves; two teachers from New South
Wales on their way to England offered to come and
help us out for the first day. Margaret Walsh—a fully

qualified teacher—decided to come out and see for herself, also to help us out. Hope has once more returned. Desks arrived at 9 p.m., a special lot at 2:30 a.m. in the morning.

Monday, 7th

School opened this morning. Mamma mia! What a day! Read about it on the other page—it deserves a special page to itself! Only ninety desks in the two schools!

Tuesday, 8th

Troubles, troubles, and more troubles! However, things are getting under control. The children, having been away from control for nine weeks, take some managing but are fast realizing that school is here to stay.

Wednesday, 9th

Amazing stupidity shown by the Public Works Department regarding our new hut. They evicted a family from a hut and found out that it was from the wrong one, but only after Tom Beasley went to remove our hut. Full of apologies about the mistake. Blew a fuse on the subject myself! Desks arrived at about 9 p.m. Frs. Nugent, Mills and myself unloaded fifty desks in pouring rain. Mother never told me about these things before I went to the seminary!

Thursday, 10th

Mud, mud, mud! How the kids love it, but what a mess!

Friday, 11th

Peace is wonderful! The savages have been tamed but at considerable cost. The Sisters and teachers are very grateful that school was over for a few days. Cheque for 171 pounds from the Cathedral as a result of our appeal—very soothing!

Saturday, 12th

We are on the move again! The new hut for Holt Street has arrived. Fr. Nugent, Tom Beasley and his men, together with some of the parishioners, prepared the hut for lowering onto the stumps and cleared out the inside. Worked savagely with two men and some boys. Got madder with each shovelful of gravel. Very good dance, people had such a wonderful time that they persuaded the orchestra to carry on till 1:30.

Sunday, 13th

Made an appeal at all the Masses at St. John's, East Melbourne, received 250 pounds for the parish. If only some of the other churches would invite us in we might be able to carry our load of debt with less agony. Returned home exhausted. Went to a meeting at Ardeer, ready to flay the parishioners. I am sick and tired of excuses. Always "Father, you must understand!" Father understands well enough and is fed up. It's about time someone else understood. Day and night the priests have slaved, worked and worried for the people and the children, it's about time some of the parishioners did their share. I have just left the meeting in disgust. Picture night to-night.

Monday 14th

Dear God, what confusion at the school. Rain pelted down. On opening the school, not one room could be occupied. The sander was still working in one room, the two rooms had been used as a hall and were filthy, and the other two rooms were packed with desks. For more than half an hour it was pure bedlam. The people must help us to clean up the rooms after dances and pictures. We must have the functions to raise money, but we could not have such a mess again.

Tuesday, 15th

Still much mud but the new slab of concrete at the back of the school is growing in size every day.

Wednesday, 16th

Frs. McSherry and Mills attended to housework and other necessary details. Fr. Nugent busy at Hold Street and visiting State Schools. Parish priest spread gravel and growled ferociously at all men passing by, found that the flat of a spade makes a satisfying sound when applied scientifically to stern of young boys who kept getting in his way! The things that don't go into this diary are much more interesting than anything written so far. Most of my readers are too young for such things so most of it will have to die with myself!

(end of bulletin)

15 February, 1955   *Melbourne*

Well! I am a bit more settled. I work, as I told you, in a Catholic school. The joke is that I teach them English, can you believe it! Me, who can hardly speak it! I am teaching all these little children (devils!) the basics of the language.

I now have my own class with forty-six boys and girls, ages five and six. This is their first experience with school. Some arrived here no more than a few months ago. I try to entertain them with stories, games and songs. Thank God I was a Girl Guide leader!

I did not know any children songs like *London Bridge* so I translated the French ones, *Frère Jacques*, *Sur le pont d'Avignon*, etc. as best as I could. I was also teaching them their prayers— the 'ail Mary full of (Canadian A) grace. When the real teacher Mrs. G. came, it was the Hail Mary full of (Australian A) grace. The poor kids must have thought that they were learning two different prayers!

The salaries in the Catholic schools are not very high, as they receive no help from the government. I earn 10 pounds (about 22 dollars) per week. Not much, but enough for me. I now live in a house with M., where we rent a room. It costs us 2 pounds (about 5 dollars) a week, with breakfast in the common kitchen included.

Our house is in St. Kilda, a suburb of Melbourne near the water. It is a sort of grey building, two floors high with long, narrow windows. With long curtains moving in the breeze, the unkempt garden and its melancholy air, it looks haunted. We share the bathroom, the kitchen and one phone, which is located in the downstairs hall.

One of our fellow residents is a tram driver. He has a fierce temper and is always barefoot. On a few occasions, he has thrown the phone at the wall because he was mad at whoever was calling him! After that, there were no calls for us for a day or two. I am scared of him and stay well away upstairs when he is on the phone!

It takes me an hour and a half to get to my class at 9 a.m. I hope God will take note of this when I get up there!

18 February, 1955   *Melbourne*

This morning the parish priest came to see my class. They sang and danced for him like angels! I was so pleased with my success that I bought myself a big bag of licorice on my way home.

14 March, 1955   *Melbourne*

Finally, C. has arrived and we are getting ready to leave Melbourne. This time it will be for a town called Alice Springs, right in the centre of Australia. We hope to see the Aborigines there, if we are lucky. We might try to find work on some farm where they raise sheep! Then we will go to Sydney. We are also thinking about going to India—the dream of a lifetime for me. C. and I must sound crazy to you.

We leave Sunday, April 2nd. If you want to know where we are going, you can trace our travels on the map. First, go west to Adelaide, then north from there to Alice Springs and then a hundred miles further north to Tennant Creek. After that we go east to Townsville, on the coast, then north to Cairns and down from there to Sydney, also along the coast—about four hundred miles all together.

The road is so bad that we will have to do parts of it by train or bus. The three of us are going. When we return to Sydney, M. will go back to Canada. C. and I will reserve passages on a ship to Singapore, hopefully in November.

Chapter 9

The Australian Outback

The idea of going to Alice Springs came to M. and I one day as we were discussing the differences and similarities between big cities. We had been in Melbourne four months and we felt that we had come to Australia to see more than just the big towns. It was decided that we would go to Alice Springs, right in the middle of the country. When C. landed in Sydney we were supposed to join her. I wrote to her about our project and she came down right away, of course.

We had met a couple of guys who had done the same trip years before. They offered to make us a tent—and gave us lots of advice. We planned to hitchhike to Adelaide, Quorn, then take the train to Alice Springs, and the road again to Tennant Creek, Townsville and Cairns. After that, we would go down the coast to Sydney. We didn't know what to expect, but with Australians being so great, we had no fear of the road.

The following is a translation of part of a diary that I kept while we were on the road in Australia. It chronicles our adventures between April 2 and May 8, 1955.

2 April, 1955

Finally we are on our way. I almost fell on the floor this morning when I tried my backpack, but it is full of absolutely essential objects. Anyway, it was too late to do anything about it. In great speed (figure of speech) we rolled down the hill to take the tram. I left our haunted house with no regrets, but not Melbourne, where everyone was very nice.

Surprise! The trams don't start before 9 a.m. on Sundays (today), and it is only 7 a.m. When they start, we miss one tram, and run for the other! I get my first sight of a sort of cowboy with high-heeled boots. I wonder where he is from! We get off at the wrong station. The street sweeper there looks at us like we are crazy, and I am starting to be of the same opinion when I look at the three of us with our bags.

The tram conductor does not take the eight pence of our fare after talking to us, but she showers us with advice. Finally we are on the road. After two years, to hitchhike again is fun—M. is not so sure yet! (She has never done it before.) Vive l'aventure!

(When I look back now, I can't get over the fact that we made it so far—and with such a lot of baggage. We had three big backpacks with sleeping bags on top.)

Unfortunately this first day, our lift leaves us in the middle of a town that is not big, but it is still a long walk for us three camels! A young Englishman and his new wife give us a ride. We have an accident, because they don't know the town. C. and I go to the police station. The duty officer asks us if anyone is hurt or dead. We say no. He loses interest. The fact that the lady whose car we hit is the wife of one of the policemen and also that the couple we were travelling with is English and may be immigrants did not bode well for them. Good luck, we say. Our duty done, we head back to the road.

Australians are very friendly towards strangers. But when they are immigrants, especially from Britain, they become impatient and refuse to consider them Australians. It must be the same in Canada, when newcomers do better than us.

Next, we get a lift of two hundred miles with two men. One is a post office employee who has read a lot and is very interesting. His friend, a fisherman, is quite the opposite. All "Japs" should be beheaded, according to him. He says Australia is for white people only!

We see some extinct volcanoes; it seems the state of Victoria is full of them, as well as many rolling hills. Sheep are everywhere and there are lots of gum trees.

Our lift leaves us ninety miles from Mount Gambier, our destination for the day. We decide to camp there, beside the road. We ask at a farm if we could put a tent up in their field. The owners are from Romania.

3 April, 1955

We are not dead but our tent is wet and we have trouble with our jewel of a little stove, which requires more attention than a poodle deluxe. Our first lift leaves us halfway to nowhere. It is warmer—a nice change as we have been frozen since Melbourne. A truck picks us up. M. and C. are in the back. There is a marvelous blue sky, gum trees, peaceful sheep and cows. Beautiful country.

Our ride leaves us in the centre of town (again) so we walk. While waiting for a lift, we go over all the dance steps we know trying to warm up. M. talks to a guy who kills rabbits and sells the skins. Rabbits are pests in Australia. Between Melbourne and Kingston, where we wait, there are special fences on each side of the road to stop rabbits from crossing and causing accidents.

We get a lift with the same people we rode with yesterday (the two young men). The land is now flat, no water, with patches of grass here and there. More often than not, there is only red brown sand, and a few lonely trees. They leave us at Meningie and a young South African picks us up. His name is Marcel and his mother is French. The four of us sing French songs, including M. who is just beginning to learn them. We sing all the songs of Charles Trenet. The weather is perfect and as we approach Adelaide we see more and more hills. We cross a lofty range with a magnificent view of the town. After the desert we passed through it is a delight for the eyes.

We had been told that Adelaide is the prettiest town in Australia. We were also told that the plans of the city had been made by a church minister and an army colonel which explains the numerous churches and pubs in the town, as well as the gardens, I suspect.

We go to the Y where we recuperate from our travels. We change out of our jeans and into respectable skirts to visit a friend of M., and barely recognize each other. We go for supper at her friend's house; I should say "tea" as they say here. Supper is tea and a snack that you take before going to bed!

4 April, 1955

We are feeling guilty because we slept at the Y. After all we have a tent! Three frozen Canadians in Australia! Incredible. A friend from Melbourne takes us to a koala farm. These little bears look just like plush toys. They eat the leaves of the eucalyptus tree, which contain enough water for them. We would like to take one with us! By 1:30 p.m., we are on the road again. One of our lifts is from a farmer who explains to us how they shear sheep—new knowledge for us. Each year, the shearers travel from farm to farm offering their services. Our friend has only a small farm of five hundred sheep. We could expect much bigger ones in Queensland and in the Northern Territories, he says.

Later that day

It is 6 p.m. and we are still waiting on the road in front of our friend's farm. He told us he hated swaggies (wandering Australians, a bit like the beggars of my youth, who went from village to village working here and there). As we feel a lot like swaggies ourselves, we can't ask to camp at his place. Luck is with us. We get a lift of two hundred miles that leaves us west of Port Augusta. The ride is lovely, in a heated car—the driver treats us to fish and chips for dinner, and we learn that he and his passenger are policemen. Since they do not know Port Augusta, we finish up at the police station. The police take us to a caravan park and look at us with amazement when we pitch our tent, and in a few minutes, unfold our sleeping bags and install the floor sheet. They ask us to promise to ask the police to help us anytime we are lost. We leave them with regrets.

It is great to be in the tent again. I think back to the Flinders Ranges that we passed, with its fantastic shapes under the moon. In the last few days we have seen plains, hills, mountains and desert.

6 April, 1955

Port Augusta I will never forget. That is where I stopped freezing. Two young men who also cooked their meals on the communal fire at the campground offer us a lift out of town. One is from New Zealand. He is a shearer. The other is English and travels across Australia working here and there.

Our luck holds. After only a few minutes we have left for Quorn with two new Australians. One is originally from Germany, the other from Yugoslavia. The German has a lot of photos of kangaroos, emus, snakes and cockatoos that he has killed while hunting in the bush!

We are not too impressed by Quorn. It feels like a frontier settlement. It seems even more so because this is where we are catching the train. We could have gone to Marree by road, but north of there our chances of rides are almost nil. We can't risk it, and since people put their cars on the train to get to Alice Springs from here, it is not good advertising for the road ahead!

After having gone north, south, east and west in the small settlement (it took us ten minutes max!) we settle down to wait for the train. We are so happy to have arrived here that we treat ourselves to a beer in one of the pubs later.

In Australia the pubs are divided into two parts: the bar for the men and the lounge for the women. What we find funny is all the women waiting outside on a bench for the men to finish their beers! They are patient. Someone told me once with a resigned air that for a male Aussie the three main interests are:

1. Beer
2. Races
3. Women

No comments!

We enter our compartment on the train, after having waited more than an hour on the dark platform lit with a few storm lanterns (there is no electricity here). We are quite surprised to find almost an entire family sharing one of the four berths in the compartment. We have the other three. We feel sorry for the woman who must share the bed with her two children. It is not an easy thing for us either. We get organized as best we can and quickly head for the dining car. We get acquainted with the people who will travel with us for the next two days, mostly Australian tourists.

We meet an engineer doing atomic research in Darwin who had been to Canada. We also talk to two English-women who hitchhike but stay in hotels. They are older than us. There is also a man who repairs and builds roofs and goes from state to state depending on the season. All are very friendly.

The moon is almost full. Outside, on the platforms between the train cars, I look at a countryside where trees are getting sparser. I am very anxious to arrive at Alice Springs.

7 *April, 1955*   *Train to Alice Springs*

Our life on the train is so interesting. I find the countryside fascinating. I tell that to everyone, all the time. We are going further and further into the desert and there are salt and spinifex bushes everywhere and that is all. Here and there a road, or rather, wheel tracks. They cross the train tracks and seem to stretch so far into the horizon that I think of the lost countries of fairy tales. Now and then we stop to take some water and we go out to stretch our legs and get to know the millions of flies of the place. They are terrible, especially at this time of the year. I don't know if we are lucky or not, but we are travelling after the rainy season, which usually lasts between one and four days a year. The desert, which is normally red and without vegetation has some "almost" green patches in April. It does not last long and everything goes back to being red and dry.

The Aborigines at the back of the train don't seem bothered by the flies. Each time we stop, some of them get off and others get on. I wonder where they come from. Here and there along the tracks there are some stone buildings, most without roofs or doors. They look abandoned. In the old days (thirty years ago maybe), I suspect the train might have stopped more often, unless these huts have something to do with the Cobb's "diligences" (stagecoaches). The poor travellers, they must have "manger de la misère" on roads that even today are not famous.

To be on a train like this gives me the same sensation that one gets on a ship in the middle of the ocean. As far as I can see on the horizon there is only salt bushes, spinifex, sometimes an expanse of white salt without water.

The interior of Australia was part of the sea millions of years ago and now, after the rainy season, we have this phenomenon of white salt lakes in the middle of the desert. Lake Eyre is usually a lake of salt, except that for the last two years, it has had water. Nature has strange ways. Nowhere else but on this train that travels miles and miles into the desert have I realized the irony of this immense country: it has no water in the interior, but is surrounded by it on all sides.

You can see Lake Eyre on the Australian map most of the time, even though for decades it has been absolutely dry. The outback is also a country of floods. During the rainy season water runs in torrents and fertilizes the earth for the months that follow. If one could control and retain the rain, one could use it more evenly and fertilize the ground. They have begun to do that near Sydney at Snowy River. But it is a very expensive project and Australia, with a population of only eight million, can't afford to do that everywhere.

I said that the train is like a ship. It is true. The people who live at the base of the low mountains we can see in the distance must envy this ribbon of light that, like an illuminated ship liner at night, transports their fellow human beings from one point to the next. It must remind them of the crowds and towns that they have left behind.

We know just about everyone on board, including an old swagman who joins us on our balcon (small open platforms at the end of each train car). I feel sorry for him—I think he is sick. These swaggies carry their sugar bags from cattle-sheep station to station, working here and there. They know where to find water in the desert, are experts on the weather and excellent hunters and fishermen!

I think of the song *Waltzing Mathilda* when I speak with our swaggie, he travels in third class on the train (we are in second). Eventually, to my chagrin, they make him go back and travel with the Aborigines.

Every evening we almost get into a friendly fight with the waiters in the dining car. They serve us what they think is good for us. They tell us about it as well. What a bunch.

From our balcon we see, here and there along the tracks, the bones of animals that died of hunger or sickness. In the moonlight they look fantastic and more and more I am beginning to imagine myself as the star of a Western movie. We sing lovely French songs that M. is starting to grow fond of.

It is our last night on the train, sad. Tomorrow, Alice Springs.

9 April, 1955

Each morning the waiter brings us a cup of tea and cookies in bed. This allows us to wait for breakfast without dying of hunger. The food is plentiful and very good. The countryside has not changed much except for a few trees here and there, and a few low hills with flat tops, all of red earth. More and more, nearby and in the distance, we are seeing herds of cattle with their drivers on horseback. Most of them are Aborigines who are good riders.

The train, as usual, is late arriving. As we can't pay for an extra dinner that costs 8 shillings (96 cents), we eat on our balcon from the provisions we have brought with us. We pass through MacDonnell Ranges and the countryside changes sharply to gum trees, grass, flowers and more importantly, to houses that are clean and have lawns.

After we arrive, I go get us some ice cream (what a luxury) while the other two go look for a policeman to find out where we can camp. When I come back everything is settled, and we are going to the police station. The only campground in the area is for Aborigines and there is no question of us camping there.

First, our friend offers us the old jail for "ladies"—we don't look too enthused. After a few minutes of consultation with his wife, he offers us the lawn of the police station, in front of the bachelors' quarters. According to him, they are all gone on holiday. He offers us the bachelors' house at the same time. Shyness makes us decline the house for a spot on the lawn and our blue tent. I have time to see a washing machine in a nearby shed; M. spots a stove and fridge in the kitchen and C., an ironing board and showers. Perfect happiness. In a very short time we are washed and have organized ourselves.

Our friendly policeman was right. The bachelors had gone, but one by one we see them come back, and we bless the Lord we had the good sense to have pitched our tent on the lawn.

The first one of our forced hosts is Ben, a young Englishman who is very nice. The others tease him because of his strong English accent. The second one to appear is Bill, who is usually posted in the outback. He has the marvelous clear eyes of the Australians from the bush, where his life is centred. That night brings us Jim, a Scottish guy from Tennant Creek who had to be forced to go on holiday. He is on his way to Melbourne. He is not happy to learn how cold it is there at the moment.

After supper in the kitchen (a real luxury), we are invited by Ben to go and visit some Aborigine trackers who live with their lubras (wives) and piccaninies (children) in the next yard, behind the post. They have caught an iguana that they are leaving to cook on the fire while they go to one of the two cinemas in town. The iguana will rest in the cinders of the fire with its four legs tied and the tail between its legs. I ask if we can have a taste of it tomorrow when it is cooked. They promise to leave us a bit of the tail.

Our first night in Alice Springs is without adventures but not without mosquitoes. We can't have everything.

C. and I go to Mass. There must be a boarding school around for half-caste, as there are many children in attendance. Two nuns accompany them. After Mass we go to say hello to the priest. He is very friendly and organizes a trip for us for tomorrow. We are to go to Santa Teresa, a Catholic mission for indigenous people. We get a ride home from a police sergeant who asks us where we are staying. To his very surprise he learns that our address is General Headquarters of the Northern Territory Police—for which he is himself responsible!

When we return home, I rush to go and get my share of the iguana. The trackers have not forgotten their promise, and cut a bit from the tail for us, the best part. The outside is carbonized but the meat itself reminds me of veal. We taste it and we would probably have enjoyed more if we had not known the origin, the cooking and the manipulation of it. I am so proud to have had a taste that our police friends don't hear the end of it.

The policeman who had greeted us on arrival is building himself a caravan in our yard. Before lunch, we have our daily talk with him. This time it is about Albert Namatjira, the famous Aborigine painter that he knows very well. He calls him "old Albert" and explains to us about the life of Aborigines who own a boomerang, a woomera, and that is about all.

After dinner, Bill, the silent one with the beautiful clear eyes, offers to bring us in his truck to where they load cattle on the train. We go, not knowing what to expect. I will never ever forget the sight of all those beasts, wild and stampeding as they tried to avoid getting on the train. The paddock where the drivers bring the cattle after many days of travel through the bush is divided into many enclosed areas, surrounded by gates that open to let the chosen animals pass through. The drivers seem to greatly enjoy making the beasts furious in these enclosed areas. They are brave—but not us—we are back at a safe distance.

Those animals are magnificent and they fascinate Bill who has eyes only for them. Most of them have never seen a man before they were gathered in a herd and driven to the selection area. After the choice is made in the midst of the dust and cries of the ones who are herding, they finally get loaded.

After this, Bill takes us to the top of a hill called Anzac. Each town or village of Australia has a monument or a hill, sometimes both, dedicated to those who died in the 1914 and 1939 wars. From this hill, we see the whole of the very pretty town of Alice Springs, which looks like an oasis between the desert we just passed through and the one that is waiting for us in the north when we leave the pass. Below us is a field where there is a match of football (soccer) between the Aborigines and some white players. We hope to be back to this hill to see a sunset as we are told it is a marvelous sight.

Back at "our" house we eat and make coffee for our hosts in their kitchen. They start talking and soon, forgetting us, they reminisce about their lives as outback law officers. It is fascinating. They talk about the rites and customs of the aborigines. The men hunt those who have broken the law—they have to. They speak about the dangers of tracking and of their nights in the bush. It makes me think about our Canadian Mounties in the far north. Their work is not for the weak and I think that one must really be "called" (if one can say that) to work and live in the Australian bush. Without mental and physical resources you would not last long.

The Australian bush is strange in that it contains few animals, but it does contain snakes, some of which are very dangerous. That evening our police friends teach us that one can love the bush so much that one can't live without it. They have to return to it after a short time away. To use Saint Exupéry's words, I would call the centre of Australia "terre des hommes."

11 April, 1955   Alice Springs

The sergeant we met at church was waiting for us and we climb on the back of his utility truck with his children. The road is really a track and we cross over many dried-up brine creeks. A week ago, water was running strong. Two men from town who wanted to cross a small river drowned in the sudden current. When it rains here, it rains. For the rest of the year, one can organize picnics, trips, and tournaments, sure of the sun.

Unfortunately the creeks, although beautiful with their gum trees, are not easy to cross and we roll from side to side "at the back." Everywhere is blue sky, red hills, spinifex, mulga trees, anthills, and mistletoe. The place we are headed for—Santa Teresa Mission—is run by Father D. He is the manager and its missionary. Five nuns also help him. He is the only white man on the station. The Aborigines work and live a short distance from the main habitation where there is a white chapel, a convent, a refectory (of galvanized iron) and a dormitory for the little girls who go to school there. Their parents live nearby in a sort of conglomeration that I don't dare call a village. It is a grouping of huts. The Aborigines live in caves or under roofs usually made of leaves. When they settle near the white people, they grab anything they can. They especially like galvanized iron, and boxes of all sizes.

The good father tries to build them small stone houses; there are a lot of stones around. He has had a lot of experience building. Before coming to Santa Teresa, he was on one of the islands north of Australia. He built a stone church that was photographed for the country papers and is especially famous for a stained glass window he made of empty beer bottles!

As soon as we get down from the truck, the flies attack us. We wear mosquito netting (around our faces) but we see with horror that the little girls don't have any and are covered by flies—eyes, nose, and mouth. They don't even bother to shoo them away.

The uniform of the school is a blue dress. They are shy girls and they hide to laugh. After our visit of the few buildings, we go in Father D.'s Jeep to visit a real village, where we are greeted by a terrible noise from all the dogs they have. The lubras are sitting down under a tree rocking their babies, in a sort of little wooden canoe, away from the heat.

Today we went to visit the flying doctors' offices. They run a radio service. They get messages for emergencies and give the weather and advice on medical matters. They also have school broadcasts. Because the families on the stations live so far from each other, they communicate among themselves and with the flying doctors by radio. This is a marvelous service. They also fly sick people to hospital emergency rooms.

We went to Stanley Chasm today. We never made it to Ayers Rock—an immense rock in the middle of the Central Australian desert. The chasm, a sort of mini-canyon, has huge orange walls and small paths. Australia is a strange land, especially around Alice Springs.

That evening, we saw the sunset from Anzac Hill—a glorious sight. Now it is time for us to say goodbye and get back to our travels.

Because there is very little traffic going north to Mount Isa (our last stop before going east to the coast), our friendly policemen arranges a lift for us on a truck going our way. To be sure that we are not left behind for what may be a long while, we go late at night to sleep in the back of the truck. We sleep under a tarpaulin and Oh boy! are we ever tired and dusty when we emerge the next morning. We feel like chicks that have just hatched. Breakfast is at Barrow Creek and the next stop is a solitary bar in the middle of nowhere where empty beer bottles are growing all around!

However, this stop has a marvelous gift for us. Right in front of the pub is a water tank on top of an enclosure for showers! We, of course, get under … fast. It was hot and dusty on the road and we are smelly from the tarpaulin—we must have used all the water they had. I am amazed they didn't send the police after us.

In this flat and dry land we are the only thing moving, just us. We are in a big truck with a trailer, on which sits another smaller truck. Our driver has deliveries to make on the way, so we stop at stations and ranches.

Jack, our driver, is quite a character. He drives barefoot and his boots are used to hold the windshields open in the cab. He doesn't say much—the only time he laughs is when he hits a snake—he shouts for sheer pleasure then! He has only a few teeth so his joy is rather frightening. We take turns sitting with him. Otherwise it is the cab of the other truck at the back—very hot and dusty.

At the bar where we had stopped earlier, Jack told us his brakes didn't work. He just slowed to a stop!

Late in the afternoon that first day, we make Tennant Creek. For some reason, the police there told us that we could not camp in town because it was not safe. I don't know why they didn't offer us a backyard. They did, however, bring us a way out of town in the direction of Mount Isa, and left us in a field by a bore. Bores (water wells with a mill and pump) are the blood of the backcountry. You can assess a station's wealth and potential by the number of bores it has.

We put out our tent beside a ravine after it is almost dark. M. is brave, but not C. and I. We are plain scared with no light. Surrounding us is only the Australian earth, the bore, the sky, and us. Our supper is not of the gourmet class. To protect us against whatever was lurking around we spray insect repellent around the tent—great protection against snakes and company!

The noise we hear is a bunch of cows going to the bore and then a couple of cars come and sweep the field with their headlights—we hold our breath!

At 4:30 p.m. the next day Jack is back, minus the second truck, but the back is now full of Aborigine families. We are glad to be on the move with him. We meet no other vehicles on these rough roads. We have a bit of breakfast in a former U.S. Army base camp, used during the war. I see a kangaroo.

We stop at a homestead where we sleep in "beds" in a very dusty house. The station is run by a manager and a group of Aborigines with women and children. They have between five and six thousand head of cattle, and ten bores on thirteen hundred square miles. The manager tells us that the company that owns the station is making good money. A while back, they were making five or six pounds per head of cattle, but now they are making twenty pounds. To make real progress, they need a railroad. I can understand their problem. Jack is a lifeline for them.

The people we meet on our homestead stops are exceptional. They have energy, are resourceful, intelligent, and so very well-mannered. A young man tells us "it is a good life for a young fellow if he has a wife." They are also very hospitable. On our second night, we have steak and onions for dinner. For breakfast, we have steak and eggs. Later, we have steak and tomatoes with three young men living and working for the post office and/or telephone company, again, in the middle of nowhere.

We pass an immense station (13,000 sq. miles) called Soudan. Visitors are not welcome, so we don't deliver there. We arrive at Mount Isa at midnight. Jack looks for a place to drop us off. We are lucky to find a lovely field and we settle down for the rest of the night.

At 3 a.m. there are flashlights in our faces! The police are looking for an escaped prisoner! They soon realize that in our sardine tin there is no room for anyone else but us. When we wake up we have another surprise. Our nice field is a small park right in the middle of town. Anybody in that small town going anywhere is passing beside our campsite. A friendly hotel owner across the street lets us use his facilities, showers as well—and we then try the road.

There was nothing we could see on the horizon going our way. We give up, sleep in someone's backyard and leave the next morning by train for an overnight trip to Charters Towers. It is a tiring but very interesting overnight trip, through a flat country that floods easily. We see cattle and sheep. Passengers tell us of their lives in Mount Isa—many men, many pubs and few women. They get money allowances (eight pounds) for working there, and save to leave.

When we get off the train on the 19th we can feel the humidity. There are tropical flowers and foliage all around. We tell our stories to our drivers and describe the anthills we have seen that are taller than us! Some people are just so nice, and we are extraordinarily lucky to meet the Cridge family that day. When they stop for us, they are pulling a small caravan and we (and our bags) squeeze in with their kids. They are going to Cairns further north on the coast.

I see sugar cane for the first time and a sugar mill as well. At night we put up our tent beside our friends' caravan. What marvelous and generous people the Cridge family was.

It is raining on the coast, but we manage to do a few things, like take a trip to an island called Green, where we see magnificent coral reefs. We also take another trip to a jungle.

On the 24th, we leave on our own to go south. The first night, we camp near a Masonic Lodge. At dawn, it is bugles and army commands that wake us up. We are near the monument dedicated to the war heroes of the Anzac wars.

After a couple of days in Townsville, with its great swimming pool, we leave for Ayr and Bowen. We sleep there in a sort of shed from a salt mill! It rains a lot.

Our next day is better. The young man who gives us a ride is alone at home. His parents are away so we cook him lunch and leave with one of his family friends for Mackay. Still raining. We only make twenty-eight miles on the 29th. The roads are terrible because of the rain and we have to push the car. We were hoping to reach Rockhampton but we can't go on—so it is a very modest hotel for us, with a visit from a pig! O Sarina!

We make Rockhampton the next day, on worse roads than yesterday, if it is possible. We had to come to a full stop in Miriam Vale because of flooding. The next day is worse all around. The water is twelve feet over a bridge so we stop right there—with quite a few other people. At 2 p.m. the next day, we can go on. Then it is Toowoomba and Brisbane in a caravan park and a treat supper at the Y. Luck is with us from there. It is surfing paradise, with the sea, and a ride of two hundred and fifty miles in one day. We pass Coffs Harbour, banana farms, beaches and Taree (with marching bands for its 100th anniversary). And finally, we arrive in Sydney.

Chapter 10

Sydney, Australia, and New Zealand

27 May, 1955   *Sydney*

I am well settled in Sydney and happy as a bird. C. and I have found a room in an attic in the suburb of Cremorne. It is full of windows and the walls are yellow. On the lower floor (our attic is in a sort of mezzanine), we share a kitchenette, a bathroom, and a washing machine with two other Australian girls.

It would be a small paradise except that it is so cold. Everyone is freezing in Sydney. They have three months of winter: June, July and August. The rest of the year, it is lovely. There is no central heating, and no fireplace, just little heaters. I will get used to it I guess. To go to work, I must go down the hill (a short walk) and take a small ferry across the bay to town, then a tram. It reminds me of my working days in Lévis.

After three weeks and many adventures, I have found a job as a director (no less!) of a playground. I begin work at 11 a.m. and finish at 5 p.m. I am free every Friday and every second weekend. It is not tiring, as there is nothing much to do. It is situated in a tough part of town, near the harbour, where houses have been replaced by factories. There are very few children around, but they make up in mischief what they lack in numbers.

We now plan to leave Sydney in December for a trip to New Zealand. We will be back in time to take a small ship to Singapore (New Guinea, Borneo, Thailand). From there we hope to take another ship for Calcutta (Penang, Rangoon). Ouf! I am short of breath just thinking about it. I have not said anything yet to my parents—I don't want to scare them!

27 May, 1955   *Sydney*

At the playground we have tea at 11 a.m., lunch at 12:30 and tea again at 3 p.m. Around 4 p.m. the children come. There are about forty of them. Our staff consists of two senior supervisors (one of which is me!) and two junior workers. The other senior is married (in his 40s) and his wife (of the same age) is my junior! The junior man is at least 35 years old, which means that I am the baby of the lot while being the boss! Nobody has had any training but they have lots of experience.

I earn 13 pounds, 7 shillings (about 22 dollars a week). It is much better than at the regular social services agencies. There they get 11 pounds or if you work for the government, 16 pounds. C. has found work there, which means that we have been very lucky.

I might try to organize some clubs, puppets maybe. I hope it goes well. I forgot to say when I spoke of our home that we have a view of the harbour. We live in a very quiet part of town, and we pay 2 pounds, 15 shillings a week for each of us. We can hear the ship horns. Marvelous! Financially, we managed to make it until now—just … but since we have our salaries, I hope to save about 4 pounds a week. After six months, I think I should have 144 pounds in the bank. With that we will go for a few weeks to New Zealand and then to India.

The funniest thing is that, last week, while waiting for an answer to my job application at the playground and not having any money left, I found work as a waitress in a restaurant! A week was more than enough for me but I gained some experience. We tried to get jobs as barmaids but the union said no way! It would have been fun and we were dreaming of all these tips we would get, not knowing that Australians don't tip!

At the restaurant, I had to count in pounds, shillings and pence. It took me forever and giving change made me quite a show in itself. Now, after a few weeks of rest, I will learn to play tennis, join a camera club, and the youth hostel.

Later that day

M. has just left for Canada. I am heartbroken. She is a super friend and travelling companion. C. is very nice, marvelous to travel with the way we do, but being so different from me, it is a bit more difficult to live together.

I must explain where and what I do to earn a living in Sydney. In Canada, when we think of a playground, we see swings, slides, sandboxes, plus trees, grass, benches, etc. Maybanke playground has none of these things. There is not much grass in the neighborhood to start out with. What we have is two levels of concrete ground, tennis-court-sized, maybe a bit bigger.

The first level is about ten feet above a retaining wall, right on the sidewalk. We have an office and meeting rooms on one level and a storage building for sport equipment on the other (the roof of which is a favorite spot for rebels—most of the kids, I would say).

They are super tough, don't like to lose, and I've had to run after them to stop them from tearing the hair of girls from a visiting team—because they had lost! They are always fighting, especially the girls, who are my responsibility. I could learn some choice swear words if I were interested. We do not always understand each other. I don't think that their English is mainstream! As for myself, they make it clear they don't understand me when it suits them.

I don't think I should have been hired. I know nothing about organized sport, which is about the only thing we can do. As a group (social) worker at home, I knew all about clubs, group activities, the dynamics of social behavior, etc., but nothing about basketball, volleyball, etc. They gave me the senior job because of my degrees and maybe in the vague hope that I could tame these kids by using psychology or something! Of course, I do have some good times and fun times with my girls.

I am greatly helped by my junior! He is a real old Irish

bachelor, built like a bear. He knows my "weaknesses" and is always around to help. We are a team. He is kind and tactful, bless his Irish soul. And here I thought I had seen little devils in St. Peter's School!

Most Sundays when I have to work, I am met at the train stop by whistling gangs of young men, who are the neighborhood greeting team. I saw a film called *Black-board Jungle*—that is my life. I never give up and I help a bit, though not in my referee duties on the basketball and volleyball courts! If you look like you can't make up your mind about points there is always someone to tell you! Without a fight it is better!

1 June, 1955   *Sydney*

I am writing to you tonight while cooking a roast. You should see the two of us as cooks!

I write so few letters at the moment that you might think writing paper is rationed here. You will laugh, but since I arrived I have had no money to buy some!

3 June, 1955   *Sydney*

The Australian Red Cross phoned and I think that they are interested in hiring me. What a joke! Their social service here is even more primitive than ours is at home. I went out this morning with a group worker who works for the government. He doesn't know much according to me ... and "me" who knows nothing! He had not much to do, I think. We went to Manly Beach in a government car. The water was so blue and the beach so white. Wonderful!

It is the beginning of winter at the moment and it is cold, not because it is so outside but because the houses are not heated—it is damp and when I go to bed I shiver. C. also—she who is never cold! In the offices it is the same thing. It is a good thing that I work outside.

Sydney is a beautiful city, built around a harbour. To go downtown and work I must take a small ferry. It is fun and that way I see a lot of sunsets.

My social life has not been too exciting. I am not complaining though. After we arrived, I worked as a waitress and I was never home in the evenings. I certainly know what it is to be broke!

I have just made some applesauce and a cup of hot chocolate. I am learning to cook, and as a consequence I might find myself a husband!

24 June, 1955   *Sydney*

I have received the maple syrup and the toffee turned sugar! Was it ever good! We are rationing the syrup and Friday I will make some pancakes. I had to go and get the whole thing at the Customs offices. They were more interested in me (French!) than in the parcel, although I had to explain what it was—what to do with it ... these Australians!

29 June, 1955   *Maybanke*

I am alone at the playground. These tough kids are so mischievous. Since I know next to nothing about team sports (or most sports to be honest), I will try to organize some clubs with the help of a university professor who is interested. I am also practicing my typing because I am looking for a temporary job as a typist. What cheek!

We get along very well with our roommates. Every night we share our daily adventures. I have just made a lemon meringue pie. It smells good. I will have it with my cup of tea. I am becoming a real old English lady!

21 July, 1955   *Sydney*

An update on our latest projects: We can't find work in India, so we will spend January in New Zealand as planned, then we will take a small cargo ship for the remaining parts of the former Dutch Indies: Papua, Thailand and Singapore. From there we hope to find a ship for Calcutta, then Bombay, Palestine and London by train! By the grace of God, I hope all goes well.

Don't think that because I don't have enough shillings and pence now and then to buy chocolate that I am destitute. So far I have saved 80 pounds and hope to save 450 pounds in the next six months. It is true that when we arrive in a new town it is a lot of hardship. But it makes us appreciate what we have afterwards.

7 August, 1955   *Sydney*

My work at the playground is not enough, so every Friday from 5 p.m. to 8 p.m. I work (again) in Cahill's, a restaurant in the Australia Hotel in downtown Sydney.

Cahill's was a posh restaurant, but the work was hard. They fed us little gray sandwiches, if that is possible, so I stole fries on my way from the kitchen. The dessert of choice was parfait—hard to steal from! Australians, the most generous of people, did not tip. I missed those tips!

I have to start making some summer dresses this week. This season is terribly hot, even reaching 108 degrees Fahrenheit! I begin work at 11 a.m. but I can use the sewing machine at the playground from 9 a.m. until then. It is a good thing that the people I work with are so nice.

23 August, 1955 — Sydney

When you say that it seems that I don't want to return home, you are right and wrong. I don't want to live in a shell but if I can find something worthwhile to do, give me Québec any day. I am anxious to return home, but not to my old life. If it does not work out I might go somewhere else—out West maybe. I will not settle down as long as I have that travel bug. I am accumulating memories and ghosts for my old age, in case I find myself all alone at 50.

As for now, I am having a great time. I don't have a boyfriend but many friends, women and men. We go to youth hostel meetings where we meet a lot of them. I went out with an Italian last week, before that a Yugoslav. There are lots of immigrants here in this country.

25 *August, 1955*   *Sydney*

The von Trapp family is here to give a performance of *The Sound of Music*. They are staying in a house nearby! Excuse me!

I gave a small talk about social work at the YWCA, in the English language of course, if you please! I am getting better. C. laughs about my accent all the time (she was from the Prairies and had no accent, French or English) We are getting along fine and more importantly we are becoming good cooks ... never a Ready Mix in our kitchen!

22 *September, 1955*   *Sydney*

Spring is here and the garden is full of flowers. I am sunburned because I work outside all the time.

Those kids at the playground are getting worse if it's possible.

Spring in our backyard means that the bananas are starting to grow and the lemons are getting yellow. Tangerines have just finished.

10 *October, 1955*   *Sydney*

We have made our reservations on the MV Sibigo which leaves on the 27th of January, 1956 for Borneo, Indonesia, Bangkok and Singapore. I stop working on the 4th of January and on the 5th we will take the plane to New Zealand. There is only a ten-pound difference between going by plane and going by boat. By working another week I save twelve pounds.

We will hitchhike in New Zealand of course. Send me a couple of plastic bags. They are useful when you travel.

This may seem like a strange request to you, but at that time it was paper bag or baskets for vegetables in Australia. In Japan you brought a furoshiki (a sort of big scarf) to the store. The salesperson put your merchandise in it and folded it neatly. I loved to see them do it. It was done with such skill and always a big smile. If what you bought was expensive, you got a pre-sento, a small gift from the owners of the little shops.

18 October, 1955   Sydney

It is spring. In a week or so I will go and get burned on one of the beaches nearby. At the moment, I am happy to sit in the backyard among the banana, lemon and palm trees. Last week I went to a youth hostel at the foot of the Blue Mountain range near Sydney. They are very blue and spectacular. I went with H. She had worked in Canada and missed it. I don't blame her.

H. was on her way back to Australia on a PO ship when she and C. became friends (the best thing she had ever done for us!) Her family and the L. family adopted us. I could never repay the kindness they showed us. Although I don't mention her all the time she was, in fact, always there for us.

Our passages are reserved for Bangkok, Singapore, etc. and we are in the process of doing the same for Singapore to Calcutta. I would like to be a millionaire, but I am in good health—that is something. We hope to be in England in August 1956, and will stay in London for a few months. Money is getting scarce after paying for all those passages, and I would like to see a lot of Europe.

I got a letter from the Canadian YWCA offering me a job in Winnipeg. They write to me wherever I go. (My "unfinished" thesis was on the YWCA in Québec City.) Will there ever be a job for me in Québec? With my 14 pounds (30 dollars) a week, I dream of good salaries back home. Nobody will want to hire a globetrotter like me. Maybe by then I will be ready to settle down.

Booking passages on the freighters was sometimes exciting and sometimes frustrating. We knew the destination we wanted, but nothing was certain for the in-between. We were never sure of the dates of departure, arrival, etc. All depended on the cargo—we had to go again and again to the shipping agent's office to know what was happening. I loved that. Going by plane, with a ticket guaranteeing you a seat and a predictable boarding time, etc. is not the same thing. Very boring!

We leave on the 6th of December for New Zealand and we return to Sydney on the 26th.

5 December, 1955   *Sydney*

Change of plans. Our ship is not leaving for another four weeks! So we leave for New Zealand on the 27th of January, 1956. As for Singapore, we will see.

We are getting ready to celebrate Christmas without

snow. Everybody goes to the beach on that day. It will feel strange. I am happy here but I would like it if you were in Sydney with me. I have so many interesting tales to tell and have met so many interesting people! Merry Christmas!

26 January, 1956 *Sydney*

That's it. We leave tomorrow for New Zealand and return on the 21st of February. Right now the longshoremen who work on the port's wharves are on strike. I hope we will still be able to leave in February!

I have done the sum of our financial resources. It will be impossible with the money we have left to go as far as Europe. So, we have decided to go to South Africa after India. If we could work in Africa for a few months, we could take the train (dream on Jacqueline!) for Europe. The trip to India is still the same. To go to Durban, South Africa, from India by ship, I will have to get what is left of my Canada Savings Bond. I need it to be able to get into the country, otherwise I won't get in or be able to get out; I will die there. Adieu Jacqueline!

They ask every immigrant to South Africa to have 100 pounds (280 dollars) on hand. Tell me what I have left and I will try to save the rest. It is very important.

I am sorry to leave Australia. We have very good friends here, I love our home in the attic and I love Australia and its Australians.

27 Jan. - 21 Feb., 1956   *New Zealand*

I didn't write much to my family and friends about New Zealand—a great country. We stayed in motor camps or, if invited (which happened quite a lot), in people's homes. C. and I were optimists: it took only one car, one lift, to move, even for a few miles, towards our flexible goals. We never intended to see everything but were ready to detour, spend another day if necessary to enjoy something new and worthwhile. As for the nights, we had a tent, and we could sleep anywhere near the road!

I could not have asked for a better companion than C. I made her laugh and she kept us focused. We were both of modest means to say the least. No rich parents anywhere.

6 February, 1956   *New Zealand*

A friend of C.'s met us on arrival and on Sunday morning we left for Wellington, stopping at Waitomo to see the famous caves. They are full of glowworms and when you look up at them you would think it was a beautiful winter sky, full of stars. From Wellington, we took a ferry to Christchurch on the South Island. (New Zealand has two main islands. We landed on the north one.)

On our way south we met a young farmer who was desperate to find someone to harvest his fruit crop. So we decided to be helpful and picked up plums for a day in Dunedin (help or hindrance!) We visited Queenstown, situated on a most beautiful blue lake surrounded by mountains.

We also went to a town called Milford Sound near a world-renowned park. Maybe it wasn't yet famous when we visited though, as there didn't seem to be any park surveillance or control in 1956.

Two guys gave us a lift to a park called Fiordland National Park. Since they intended to leave their car and hike further, we decided to pitch our tent in an immense rocky valley, beside the only tree growing there and a small creek. There was nothing but small rocks and pebbles around us. No wonder—we learned on the return of the hikers that our tree was the only one left in the valley after the constant rock slides there. What you don't know sometimes does not scare you but after freezing to death in our blue tent we were glad to be out of there.

Later in February, 1956   *New Zealand*

New Zealand is very different from Australia, which is a very dry country. Here it makes me think of Canada or England as I imagine it. The farms are lovely and the hills full of sheep. This morning I have seen snow for the first time since Mount Fuji in Japan. It is very cold and C. and I would love to have mittens.

New Zealanders are so nice! When we return to Christchurch we will go and climb a glacier called Franz Josef near Greymouth on the west coast, then visit Picton and take the ferry back to the north island. We hope to visit Rotorua, where there is a Maori village. After that we take the plane which will bring us back to the strike!

These Australians! We were supposed to leave Sydney on the 27th of February but we might have to wait a while!

26 February, 1956   *Sydney*

I am back in Australia, safe and sound. It is now my second home! Because of the strike, our ship is expected to leave on the 4th of March. We should be in India in the middle of May. From there we will leave for Durban and Johannesburg. I have written to our "attaché d'affaires" there. He answered that there are lots of jobs available and it is easy to enter the country.

While waiting for our ship, we are staying with H.'s sister and her husband. We leave tomorrow for a stay of a few days on a sheep station near Brisbane, with another of H.'s sisters. Will we ever leave!

Chapter 11

MV Sibigo

13 March, 1956   *MV Sibigo*

We finally left Sydney last Thursday, March 8th, at 2
p.m. Our ship is quite small (2,185 tons). When we were
looking for it last Wednesday in order to deposit our luggage (two small suitcases, two battered backpacks with
exhausted sleeping bags on top!), the commissioner at
the entrance to the piers directed us to the "submarine"
as he called it! Submarine or not it floats, but I must admit that it looked invisible beside a Pacific Ocean liner!

I was seasick for the first couple of days on board. Just
to shame my sailor ancestors. Now I am okay. This is a
Dutch ship with six Dutch officers and a crew of a dozen
or more Chinese (Indonesians). Everyone is very nice.
We have just finished doing some exercises on our only
small deck. I am also learning some Dutch.

We will stop four times in Dutch New Guinea—at Hollandia, Biak, Manokwari, and Sorong. In British Borneo, we will stop at Sandakan and Jesselton. Then, on to Bangkok, Singora, and Singapore, which will be our last port of call. Many of these places are on islands.

While I think of it, I must tell you about the fantastic people we stayed with in Australia while waiting for our ship to arrive. H., our great friend, arranged for us to stay at her sister P.'s sheep station, north of Sydney, on the border of the states of Queensland and New South Wales. We hitchhiked there and back. P. and her family treated us like long lost friends. We slept, ate, went horseback riding, had tea and then more tea—a great restful holiday. On our first morning, we awoke to thumping on the floor. It was a baby kangaroo going out through our room! It had been found in the pouch of its dead mother and been raised as a pet.

On our return to Sydney, while waiting once more for our ship, we stayed with another sister of H. When we finally left, we got flowers from the L. family. They are marvelous, generous friends. My junior at the playground in Sydney and K., also a friend, came to see us off.

Well, Australia is a thing of the past now. I left with regrets. Good things don't always last. After this we will head to Africa. What do you think of that? Don't forget that we don't arrive in Singapore until the 20th of April.

I am now in Sandakan, our first port in Borneo. We leave tonight for Jesselton. In Hollandia we stopped for a full day, and had a party on board. In Sydney we might have looked like a submarine, but in these little ports we were a big ship and a great social event for the community.

Afterwards, we went to the Navy Commissioner's house for dinner, a rice taffel (little Indonesian dishes with rice). It was delicious.

In Biak, we went to take photos in a nearby village where we saw former (I hope) headhunters, then we went swimming with the ship's officers in a lagoon also near us.

In Manokwari we visited the town by car. It is something to see the local fashion! Just get one and a half yards of cotton and wrap it around yourself.

One of our fellow passengers had worked for Royal Interocean and its predecessor, KPM. This trip was a kind of thank you for all his years of service. He got the royal treatment everywhere, and being a generous Australian, he invited us poor Canadian girls to join him most of the time.

In Sorong we visited the little town and crossed to the island of Doom! We walked around with a young Dutchman. He had big blue eyes, blond hair and moved like a tiger! He is a painter and is interested in archaeology. Wow!

After seeing the island, we came back to the ship for a party. At midnight we went swimming in the lagoon with some of the officers, and then we left the next day. Since then the sea has been calm and the moon is full. The sunsets are out of this world.

I don't know what the rest of the trip will be but so far it has been marvelous. The ports of Dutch New Guinea are not so well kept up as the ones of Borneo. It is only since the war that Holland and Australia have been looking after them. In New Guinea, the population is dark brown and black. Their hair is curling so tight around their heads that it looks like a crown. They are very small and wear sarongs, sometimes just a loincloth (a bikini sarong for men!)

Here in British Borneo there are no more black people, but Dusun, who are similar in appearance to the Malay people. They dress in pyjamas like the Chinese and wear the famous coolie hats. They are clean and polite. Junk boats are all around us.

We went to a Catholic mission this morning for a visit. It had a very pretty church.

The little plush dog you sent me is in the chart room where he has become the pet of the duty officers. The captain treats us like daughters and looks after us like a mother hen!

We stayed only a few hours in Jesselton and did a bit of shopping. Did I tell you that at Sandakan we saw an Indian snake charmer that was a magician as well? I understood nothing but I laughed a lot … which says a lot for his power of communication. Also, with the ship officers, we tried the local beer. It was a German type (a big surprise). Then we went to the barber, the officers on the men's side and me on the women's side, all of us sheared like sheep!

Ask the uncles (the ones that are river pilots) about the Dutch ships they have worked on. This one is clean and everyone is so very polite. Does the name "Bols" (a drink) mean anything to them?

Here is a breakdown of my days on board the ship. I am up between 6:30 a.m. and 7 a.m. Then I go to the bridge to chat with P. (the first officer), or T. (the second officer). I go up for breakfast at 8 a.m. After breakfast I read, write, and sew. I bought a cheap sarong that I like very much. I also play mah-jong. At 10 a.m. it is time for morning tea. Sometimes I play chess with the off-duty officers. At 1 p.m. we have lunch. Most of the time I go to sleep on the deck with my pillow in the afternoon. At 7 p.m., dinner is served. Then it is mah-jong, chess, talking on the bridge, looking at the stars, drinks, coffee, and bed.

At the beginning of the trip, we did exercises in the morning with F., the second engineer. Now he plays bridge — thank God!

Even if it appears to be a dull life, the least little event assumes great importance. At Easter, for example, the captain gave each of us women a chocolate egg. After lunch we had an egg hunt all over the bridge and the deck. We were like kids, C. and I. We found one each. That night we had drinks after dinner in the captain's cabin. It was a great Easter.

When I was going to school as a little girl they were teaching us the names of the big seas of the world. Who could have predicted that one day I would cross the Coral Sea, the Gulf of Siam and the China Sea, and here I am two days from Bangkok with some islands of Cambodia on the horizon.

Our trip is a dream come true. There are only seven passengers on board: two couples, a young American, and the two of us. We are a very small family. The captain is a darling and the officers too. Except for those few days at the beginning, I have not been seasick at all. Right now it is hot and the sea is like oil.

It was so hot last night that I went to the bridge and B. (the American) gave me a whole lecture on Greek mythology, which I soon forgot. Then it was the turn of the sky and the stars. Right now we can see both the Southern Cross and the Polar Star.

I have to say something about B. He joined us at Hollandia on his way to Singapore. He was in the import/export business. So he said! Now I think that he was a CIA agent. He never said a word about business or what he did export or import!

We had only one main room on the Sibigo. It was the dining room, lounge, dance and party room, reading room, etc. During the day and for most meals, we were in shorts and sandals. It was very informal. At night, however, it was different. We put on our "unique" and only "skirts"—and the officers that we thought looked quite neat already during the day had to be in spotless whites. We had a menu! And it was quite formal. B.

came to his first dinner in shorts and sandals. The Captain told him to dress up, but the poor guy had no long pants and no socks, so he and the "boss" compromised! Shorts, plus a loan of a pair of the captain's long white socks. They became great friends, B., the tall American (over 6 feet) and the small captain (5 foot 6, I think). The captain was the supreme master of our ship and of our lives, so we had to do what he told us! It is always so at sea.

6 April, 1956   *Sibigo at Siam*

We will be in Bangkok tonight, then Singapore. I would like it very much if the ship was to come with us everywhere but when it leaves Singapore it goes to Hong Kong, Shargnan and Grentsin. If I were rich I would go with them. One can't have everything!

6 April, 1956   *Bangkok*

At about 9 p.m. we see in the distance the lighthouse at the entrance to the Chao Phraya River. At 10 p.m., after we pass the last buoys of the canal, we take a pilot. He is Siamese, short, with a perpetual smile. The Gulf of Siam is calm and warm. With no breeze, the river is still. Alongside the other passengers on the bridge, we look from side to side of the river. We see houses on piles and sometimes a temple with its elegant tower, pointed to the sky.

We must stop to greet the Customs officers. When we approach the town, it seems engulfed in flames. I wish you could have seen it. The pilot tells us that a big market is on fire. The light from the flames gives us an idea of the spread of the town. We fill out form after form at Customs. Then I go back on the bridge. I can't see anything but silhouettes. The night is so dark; there are no stars.

At midnight we are in Bangkok—at least on the wharf, where we fill out more forms, then go to bed at 2 a.m. After breakfast all of us seven passengers go ashore with the captain, who takes us to tour the town which is about four miles from the wharf. We go to his company office first. Then, in their station wagon, we go to see the Temple of the Reclining Buddha. It is the first of a series of marvels that we will see.

The Buddha of Wat Pho must measure about one hundred and fifty feet in length and fifty feet in height. He is made of plaster around a brick core and is covered with gold leaf. The soles of his feet are inlaid with inscriptions in mother-of-pearl—which list the qualities of a good Buddhist. We eat at the Hotel Europe, then the two of us go to meet P. at the Trocadero Hotel. We have the surprise of our life to see the second officer with him. They have put on ties and white shirts and we are very proud of our two Dutchmen even if their height of six feet plus forces me to tilt my head towards the sky when I look at them!

We go see a film, then we meet three Siamese friends of P. who invite us to go and have a Siamese beer with them in a Siamese restaurant. They drive us through the Chinese part of town and it seems to me to be as lively at night as it is during the day. They are very nice and extremely polite.

We go to town again with the captain. As he wants to shop, we are looking forward to visiting those marvelous stores we saw yesterday. This time we succumb to temptation. C. buys some silk and I, a stole, which is beautiful. We have lunch at the Oriental Hotel with B. and the captain. On the way, a jeweller almost grabs us. He wants to show his precious stone collection. Brother! If only I was rich—opals, sapphires, diamonds, emeralds, etc. We buy nothing of course! We finally sit down to eat at 2 p.m. and when we return to the ship at 5 p.m. the sunset on the river is wonderful. On each side are coconut trees and bamboo houses on piles.

At 8 p.m., we leave with one of the couples and the captain to go around the nightclubs of the town. We have dinner at a Hungarian restaurant. Then we go "Chez Eve" "Club 88", "The Oasis," and "The Bamboo Bar." We are back home around 1:30 a.m. Ouf!

P., the first officer, has a Chinese friend here named Mr. W. He is a businessman who also looks after the loading and unloading of the ships in port. Mr. W. asks P. if he could be of service to him and P. suggests that he show C. and I the town. The best idea of his life as far as we were concerned.

At 6 a.m., with our eyes barely open, we leave with him and Sparks, the telegraph and communication officer. First we go to the floating market, Mahanak. Bangkok has been named the Venice of the East because of the numerous canals that criss-cross it. In some of these a market is held everyday. The sellers have their merchandise in a small boat and to shop, you paddle around them in a small boat as well.

Mr. W. rents a motorboat and we go from one canal to the next, and under bridges where there are still more markets. On the banks of the canals, people prepare their breakfasts, brush their teeth, swim, and wash their sarongs, dishes and themselves all in the same water that receives their "surprises." The water is gray but you will laugh when I tell you that we both breathe deeply and fill our lungs. The air is full of the scent of the flowers that are growing everywhere, and we enjoy it like children.

People smile and salute as we pass. Some look like dolls with their hair half-shaven. Our host buys us two hats each—one Siamese and one Chinese. More luggage!

After the market, we return to the river Chao Phraya, which crosses the city. Then we go to see the Temple of the Dawn. The Siamese have great taste for colour. This temple is on the shores of the river. Constructed by a king of Chinese origins, the temple's decorative dragons and people are Chinese. Around the main tower there are four chedis (towers). From the very top of the highest chedi, you can see a long way and get a good idea of the town. There is a palace in front, and you can see the chedis of other temples.

We return to the quay from which we had started and then go to the Temple of the Golden Buddha. The colours are so rich—gold and blue shine in the sun. I believe that I am the heroine of a fantastic tale. We are lucky that today is a national holiday and this temple is open to the public. There is also another temple dedicated to the ashes of the first king of the present dynasty (eight generations), which is open only once a year.

Mr. W. buys flowers, small medals and pictures for us. We put the flowers at the feet of the Buddha and we sit on our heels in front of the statue. While the people worship, we look around trying to absorb everything. Contrary to the Japanese, who have sumptuous tastes and whose kings spent lavishly on gold and precious stones, the Siamese are simplicity itself.

After visiting Wat Phra Keo (Emerald Buddha), we go to see the Standing Buddha, a statue of one hundred feet. I forgot to say that after our boat ride we went for breakfast at the Rattanakosin Hotel, the best in town. The government runs it.

Next, we went to see the Golden Buddha. A century ago, there were four of them in Siam. When Cambodia invaded Siam, the monks hid these immensely valuable statues. Only two have been found. The one we are going to see was found last year after forty years in cement. The temple is modern, not the traditional Siamese at all, but the Buddha (ten-twelve feet) is impressive.

Now we are going to the Marble Temple, and here I thought I had seen the best! Imagine a temple made of white marble with a border of golden tiles around the doors and frescoes made of blue tiles. Boy oh boy! J'ai le souffle coupé. It is so beautiful; we have no idea at home of the splendour of these temples. It is not made of cheap stuff, but the best marble, gold, emerald, jade and silver. The next temple houses bronze Buddhas from all over Siam and neighbouring countries. I like Buddha.

Our next visit is to the shop of a Siamese silver merchant. On our way we pass the Royal Palace where Mr. W. points to stables that house two white elephants used by the king for his coronation. That must be something to see!

The silver merchant is a friend of Mr. W. We go to the back of the store to the workshop to see what is going on. Everything being made here is silver of course, and it is so well done. We have the surprise of our lives when Sparks buys us a pin each—what a sweetheart! After all this we go for lunch in a Chinese restaurant. The menu is soup, meat on little sticks, fried rice, beer and iced tea. I eat with chopsticks—I have not forgotten how.

At 4 p.m. we return to the ship. We want to see some Siamese dances and Mr. W. promises to send us a rickshaw to take us to the market that is ten minutes from here. All the officers are working. To our great surprise, the Siamese friend that we met the night before comes to get us with a French coupé car. We feel like two "pashas" going through the town.

We go to the Sandhikorn theatre. From the street, one can hear strange sounds from within. What music! We are going to see a drama called *Imao*. There is singing and dancers just like in the pictures of our youth. The dancers are women. They are pretty, like dolls. They wear brocade costumes full of precious stones. They move like the silver bracelets we saw in the silver factory; they are so graceful that even though I don't understand a thing, I follow their movements with pleasure.

The orchestra is right beside us. It is made up of three xylophones (two bamboo and one metal), drums, gongs, a little flute and a tom-tom. According to me, the singers sitting beside the orchestra are off-tune! Though the music here seems to have more of a tune than in Japan. When I mentioned that to C., she looked at me for a full two minutes as if I was crazy! Then she really laughed! What I said must have been really funny. It was not Beethoven for sure!

After the theatre, we took a rickshaw with a motorized bicycle. When I think that I am in Siam it feels like I am dreaming.

We are now sailing in the Gulf of Siam. Tomorrow we stop at Singora on the west coast of the Malay Peninsula to load some teakwood. Then we leave for Singapore.

Bangkok was one of the places in the world that I most wanted to see. I was pleased that I saw such a lot, and I am pleased to have done the same here thanks to Mr. W. and P., the first officer, my friend.

12 April, 1956   Singapore

We are safe and sound in Singapore. When we first got here, we stayed two days on the ship and then they left. I can't begin to describe how sad we were to see them go. We cried a lot!

We have been very busy since then. I try not to think back. We arrived on the 12th, and on the 14th we moved to the YWCA. We will leave here on the 30th for Penang, Rangoon, and Calcutta. Contrary to the original plan, we will come back to Calcutta from Bombay to take a ship for Durban. It will be a ship like the Changsha with room for passengers. We will stop in Madras and Colombo I think.

I can't quite say the same of Singapore as of Bangkok. The town is on an island situated at the lower tip of the Malay Peninsula. Raffles, a visionary Englishman, realized the quality of the port and its strategic location. He acquired the island for the "Empire" and certain commercial interests in 1819. From a swamp, a town was born. It is a strange city with an even stranger population. There is no temple and the buildings are neither old nor modern. The inhabitants are Malay, Indian, Chinese, and Indonesian. It is a real melting pot. Here, there is a bit of everything.

The white population, who ruled like masters here, lost power and wonder when they will have to leave. Singapore is a free port. One finds everything here, but it is not as good as Hong Kong.

Boy oh boy! It is hot in this place. And it will be worse in Calcutta. Send me a bit of Canadian snow!

We are leaving for town in a few minutes. We sleep in the afternoon, as it is too hot to move. In the morning we push ourselves to go out. At night we go out with B., our American friend and some officers of the Sibigo who are waiting to go back to Holland. I have made a friend with an officer of the same shipping company. His ship is even smaller than ours!

Chapter 12

MV Santhia RMS

30 April – 11 May, 1956

The British ship we took to go to Calcutta was very differ-ent from the Changsha and the Sibigo—it had well-divided and strictly-enforced classes. We were in second class of course, and the passengers were mostly Indian. The ship first stopped in Penang, which was a beautiful city. We visited Kek Lok Si Temple in Ayer Itam, Penang Hill, and a snake farm of which, thankfully, I remember nothing....

4 June, 1956   *Rangoon*

I intended to tell you all about Rangoon and India as I went along, but I lacked the energy to do it. Now that I have the time, I will recount to you what happened there ... the main things, that is.

I would like to introduce you to Rangoon. If you look on the map you will see that Siam and Burma are beside one another. The Burmese are of Mongolian descent. They look like the Siamese, but what a difference there is between the two countries! I should not judge by one town but I have done it before so here it goes....

We arrived in Rangoon on the 5th of May, around noon. We stayed anchored in the harbour until 3 p.m. We decided to take a short walk around the port.

I can't begin to describe how dirty it was there; the state of the streets was terrible. There was garbage everywhere, and the pavement was broken. People looked very unkempt. I won't mention the red stains left from people spitting betel nuts, or the souvenirs left by animals in the streets. I had been hoping to find another Bangkok, but I was very disappointed.

Now and then we saw pretty Burmese girls with their hair tied up in buns. They wore short jackets and floor-length sarongs, tied at the waist. The men dressed like they do at home. Our walk was very short because of the mud and water on the ground. There was nothing much to see except vendors selling meat full of flies. It did not smell too good either. We were also told that there were thieves everywhere! Not a very welcoming country it seems.

Malvin, a young Burmese man we had met on the ship, took us to see the tallest pagoda in the world. It was a glorious sight. Since it was covered in gold, it shone in the light like a small sun. In the alleys that led to the pagoda, there were merchants selling flowers and religious items. And there were beggars every step of the way. Since Buddhists do not kill animals, there were also dogs and more dogs, many thin and sickly-looking. It broke my heart.

The main pagoda had other monuments around it; they were placed at random it seemed. In Bangkok some of the temples seemed neglected, but in Rangoon they were decrepit and didn't have the beauty of their Siamese brothers.

After a tour of the town, we went to Malvin's house to have lunch with his family. On the way, we saw some nice parks and a couple of lakes. Malvin's father is a judge. In fact, we know all the members of the family, since we travelled with them on the Santhia. Lunch is the main meal and consists of curry and rice. Indians use a lot of spices in their curry. In Burma it seems they make it with different ones—a bit hot for us but it was very good.

After lunch, we went to see the university and then a big hall in a cave that could accommodate two thousand people. That was where they held the Buddhist "synod". When we arrived, a monk was singing a prayer. Other monks, dressed in orange, responded. There were people sitting in the centre on the floor and the monks were on raised steps around them. I think that the crowd was more interested in us than in the service!

Later, we went to see some Burmese dancers in a park. Their dances looked a lot like the Siamese ones, but were livelier. They moved their arms when they danced, whereas in Thailand, the dancers tended to move just their hands.

Malvin is fifteen and very Americanized in his manner. His family was very friendly with the British during the protectorate. At that time, Burma was more or less peaceful and Rangoon was one of the cleanest towns in South East Asia. Now the countryside is full of bandits. It is not wise to go further than twenty miles from town. Only the capital and the town of Mandalay are under the government's control. To go to Mandalay (north on the Irrawaddy River) you must take an armoured boat. The only temporary stability in the countryside is maintained by rivalry between bandit groups. The Burmese we met were so nice, polite, and generous that it really is too bad.

Our next day in Rangoon, we spent shopping "with our eyes." We saw the bazaars and had lunch with two other Burmese passengers. In the evening, one of our second-class passengers gave a piano recital. After the concert, two other Burmese passengers invited us to Chinese food in the Chinatown.

I don't want to come back here. It is too bad, as we have made good friends.

In Penang, we picked up a group of Gurkha soldiers with their families. These men from Nepal were, and are, renowned for their courage. They are fierce fighters and were famous all through the British Empire. Their cabins were in the same hallway as ours (the cheapest part of the ship, need I say).

Before we left to go ashore on our second day in port, we noticed that all the brass railings around us were covered with washing that had been set out to dry by the soldiers' wives. We came back later to the beginning of the Third World War. Somehow, thieves had got on board while we were away (we had been warned of this possibility) and had stolen all the clothes off of the railings. The Gurkha soldiers (in different stages of dress!) were running around brandishing dangerous-looking knives and shouting what must be swear words in Nepali! I was glad not to be a suspect. Even more glad that we had locked our cabin door.

The wives of these soldiers had big golden rings on their noses. I was fascinated with them, their jewellery (massive and valuable, I am sure), their way of dressing (not quite the Indian way) and their lovely babies.

The Changsha and the Sibigo had been spotless. The Santhia, in second class, was not. We had a sort of plum pudding for dessert every day and there were only a few deck chairs—showing clearly the spot where people's heads had been resting. A lot of oil was the fashion.

One evening, I met a young Englishman, a botanist, who had discovered new plants. He was very, very boring, but when he said that he now had to give names to all of the discovered species, I told him to use mine! Is there a *Jacquelinus* green thing out there?

Chapter 13

Kashmir, India

This long letter was written in the spring of 1956 in Pahalgam (Kashmir). It describes my adventures in India and Kashmir between the 19th of May and the 9th of June.

6 June, 1956   *Pahalgam (Kashmir)*

I continue my story. I am sitting in front of our small tent that belongs to this missionary camp here in Pahalgam. This morning I did laundry again. We have so few clothes that we have to wash almost every day. The nylon blouse that you sent me is a treasure. I also made myself, mostly by hand, a red skirt and the three of us, blouse, skirt, and I, spend most of the time together! Never mind, when I come back and get rich that will change! To see the Himalayan peaks all around us is worth a bit of hardship.

I am too lazy to take the table out of the tent so I am writing on my knees. Now I will get on with my story.

May 11

We docked in Calcutta's harbour around 12:30 p.m. We did not go ashore until 6:30 p.m. We were already stunned by the heat. It was a real battle to get and control a couple of coolies to carry our luggage to the YWCA.

One of the best legacies left by the British in India was the number of YW and YMCAs all around the country. They were safe, reasonably-priced havens for us. Most were located in colonial buildings with high ceilings, fans and big verandas. They were also centrally located. They had dining rooms with plain food. It was mostly English food, except in the south of the country. In one Y down there, they had no forks—just chapatis and Indian curries. The curry was so hot that we were given bananas at each meal. Water does not help that kind of fire! In that residence, we had a huge white-walled room to ourselves with canopy beds and mosquito netting. Regal is a good word to describe it.

May 12

We are in Calcutta. Today was a Muslim holiday. We went to a theatre to see some traditional Indian dances in the morning. We were back before noon, hugging walls and anything that offered shade, as it was burning hot. The rest of the day we spent in bed. It was an effort to even move. Only in the evening did we go out for a walk. There were cows everywhere, in the streets, on the tram tracks, and on the sidewalks, and they were eating whatever they could find.

The Y was in the centre of town, but we were too hot to look around the city very much. We noticed lovely Indian women in their saris, or in pyjama-like outfits (large baggy pants, embroidered tunics and a scarf to cover their heads). Many of the men wore turbans. Sunday we went to Mass then read in bed! It was too hot!

Tuesday, we left for Benares by train in third class. We were packed in like sardines. It was very hot and dusty, with lots of soot from the locomotive coming in through the open windows, along with more heat! It was an overnight train and we sat all night. It was a slow start as cows were sitting along the train tracks.

Wednesday, we arrived in Benares very dirty and exhausted. We met a priest on a bike. He glanced at us and took off when we tried to speak to him! That night we stayed in a small hotel, as there was no Y. We could not breathe for the heat, so we locked ourselves in our room waiting for the coolness of the late afternoon.

At 5 p.m., we got enough courage to go out. We went by rickshaws (the poor guys!) to see some temples and a very famous Buddhist site. We had been told that there were some Canadian missionaries not far from the hotel so we went to visit them. They were seven priests of the Capuchin order from all over Canada. The priest we had scared in the morning was their superior! They gave us some coffee and we had a good time.

Thursday, we got up at 4:30 a.m. to leave and saw people bathing in the river Ganges. It does not look as dirty as one might think, but it would take a million dollars to convince me to put my big toe in it! Here and there we saw holy men getting ready to pose for the day, some on their heads! The streets were thick with pilgrims, children, merchants and the curious, like us. Benares is a sacred place for Muslims and Hindus. Later, we looked at some temples where unbelievers (us) are forbidden to enter.

We also went to a store where they made and sold saris. It was like being in the tale *A Thousand and One Nights*. We were surrounded by silk saris in marvellously beautiful colours.

We decided that we had to put a stop to the "resist the urge to buy" state of our lives.

Of course, we didn't have money, but the merchant told us that we could each have one and pay later. He trusted us! We didn't need any encouragement.

I chose an old rose one with lots of gold-embroidered cornucopias and a beautiful palu. C. bought a green one. We paid when we got our first salary in Durban.

I still own mine. It is made of the best silk in India.

May 17

Yesterday, we left for Lucknow by train (third class). When we arrived there at 5 p.m., we went straight to the Y to collapse. That night we slept on the roof-terrace of the residence. All around, we could hear the sound of the city: songs, flutes, strange music, and the noise of the bazaar. It was an exotic lullaby for a beautiful warm night under the stars.

May 18

Today we left for Kanpur and Delhi in second class. It was not too bad this time.

The countryside is always the same: dry brown plains. The houses are low, and made of mud. They are usually in small groups or clustered into villages here and there. It is hard to distinguish them from the land, as they are the same colour. We saw a few trees, and veiled women carrying water jugs on their heads. Sheep and water buffaloes roamed with their keepers, just like in the Bible. We saw wells with cattle circling round and round them, pulling the well bucket up. There were small Hindu temples with little red flags. Dust covered all that we saw—dust from the dry land that will become very fertile once the monsoon arrives in a few weeks. However, we were too early—we arrived smack in the middle of the hot season. It is at least 120 degrees Fahrenheit in the shade, I've been told!

May 19

We travelled at night from Delhi to Pathankot, a town that borders Kashmir. We caught the bus to Srinagar at 9:30 p.m. with just a few minutes to spare. We'd been dreaming of cold weather ever since Calcutta and were hoping it was waiting for us in the north.

We had lunch at Jammu, a small town with awful winding streets. Then we were en route for a pass where we spent the night. The road was tortuous to the extreme. Mountains and cliffs were on one side, precipices and cliffs on the other. Heavy military traffic shared the narrow road with us.

We climbed to 5,000 feet, 7,000 feet, then 9,000 feet. By this time, we were freezing. In the late afternoon, we reached the Banihal pass at 9,290 feet altitude. It led to the Srinagar valley. At this elevation, pine trees surrounded us—they made us homesick.

We were lucky and found two beds in the dak bungalow. The dak bungalows are rest houses scattered all over India that were built by the British for their travelling civil servants. The bungalows are now the property of the Indian government. It cost us only one or two rupees (about 20 cents) to stay in this one and it was very clean.

May 20

We left our bungalow at 4:30 a.m. At 11 a.m., we went through a tunnel and shortly after we were in the Srinagar valley.

The town was in a fertile valley full of rice paddies, lakes and beautiful rivers. It was strange to find myself in a valley at 5,000 feet altitude. The Srinagar valley was cool at this time of the year, making it an ideal escape from the burning sun of the Indian plains.

When we arrived at the tourist office in Srinagar, we learned that we would not be allowed to camp in or near the town. In order to consider our options, we decided (not much choice!) to go to a hotel. The cheapest room was up on the third floor. They put mattresses on the floor and it was like camping at tree level!

We were anxious to see the town and the lake, so we took a tonga (horse-drawn carriage) back to the tourist office.

A man started to run after us. He said his name was Abdul. He owned one of the beautiful houseboats that lined the shore of the lake. He had two people staying in it, but wanted two more to help share the cost (and profit!)

We understood him to say that the current tenants were father and son. We would not pay more than what the hotel was charging us.

It sounded too good to be true, but we decided to have a look. We thought that we could never afford it!

It was paradise. A little palace on the water! It had three bedrooms, a dining room, a living room, and a terrace on the roof with lounging chairs, tables and lots of flowers in big earthenware pots. The terrace had a roof itself, with long white drapes hanging down to keep the sun off.

Besides the main houseboat, there was a small plain one for cooking and washing in. Did I mention that it looked like a dream come true?

The houseboats themselves were moored and could be reached by land. But the action was on the water. Shikaras brought food, flowers, and merchandise to the little steps in front of the boat. During the day, the lake was busy with all these merchants. At night, the lake was still.

We went to meet the other occupants. We found out that they were not father and son, but two English engineers on leave from the Persian Gulf! They were slightly older than we were, and very nice and polite. We negotiated the arrangement and the next morning we moved in. We had certainly not planned or even dreamed of this. Neither had the two Englishmen.

The next day, our hosts confessed that they had been getting very bored by themselves. They invited us to go trout fishing with them (what fun!) We also went to Gulmarg where we went horseback riding on an old polo field at 11,000 feet, in a valley surrounded by mountains!

Then, after some discussion, we decided to go with our two new friends, Abdul, and the members of his family on a five-day caravan trek into the mountains, off the beaten track. We were told that very few tourists went where we were going.

During our trek (and for the first and last time in my life), I climbed to the top of a mountain pass, where I could see a lot of snowy peaks in front and around me. I will never forget it. I was level with some of those mountain peaks. I have seen the beauty and the splendour of the Himalayas from the roof of the world.

The pass was maybe 12,000 or 13,000 feet high or more—for me it was Everest!

We stayed on the houseboat until our friends left. Then we returned to Pahalgam to camp. Tomorrow we leave for the plains, and the heat.

I will never forget Kashmir. Not only have we seen what everybody has seen—Srinagar, the lakes, and the gardens—but we had the incredible luck to be able to camp, climb and enjoy the mountains. We had a good time, and felt as if we were the children of millionaires.

What have we done to be so lucky?

Two young girls, missionaries from the camp we are staying at (a holiday tent camp for missionaries), have invited us to visit them after we see Delhi, Agra, and the Taj Mahal. First, we will go to Bombay for a few days, then back to Calcutta, or else down to Colombo to board our ship. When you get this letter I will probably be in Africa!

Looking back on our stay in Srinagar, I can't believe that we accepted at face value that we would, with our modest contribution, share half the cost of a houseboat! Especially such a luxurious one as the Highland Queen! And our stay in Kashmir involved somewhat more than I told my family....

As I wrote home earlier, we initially thought that Abdul had found a father and son to rent half of his houseboat. It made sense that more occupants would help reduce the cost of rent and increase his profit.

After searching all over the lake for that family, we discovered, to our surprise, our two young English engineers on leave from their oil company in the Persian Gulf.

They were bored: it is true. They probably asked Abdul to find them some company, and two Western girls travelling alone must have seemed to be a gift sent from Allah! The two of us, after some discussion with Abdul and the engineers, managed to convincingly argue that we couldn't pay much. That was okay by them, so we all decided to give it a try.

That first night, the evening was young, and our two new friends invited us to go out on the lake in shikaras. These are flat-bottomed wooden boats that are quite long and narrow, with a pointed front and back. In the centre there was a big cushion and some pillows to sit and lean on. It was very comfy. These boats also had a sort of canopy with curtains that could be closed. A man with some sort of heart-shaped paddle sat at the back of the shikara, moving it along.

I found myself sharing a shikara with G. as we made our way around the lake. For the first time in my life, I almost became an instant saint. G. and I had a misunderstanding, and I said that I would jump into the lake. Since I can't swim, I was well on my way to earn a halo! We reached an "entente cordiale" and became good friends. During our stay at the houseboat we often went around the lakes in "silent shikaras."

On those nights, we enjoyed the stillness of the lake and the beauty of the night. We were surrounded by mountains, with the full moon thrown in for good measure. On his harmonica, G. would softly play all the songs we loved. It was magic, pure magic. It seemed we were alone in the world. After our first night on board, G. and A. invited us to go trout fishing. We caught nothing, but it was fun to try. We ate our lunch on the banks of a fast-running mountain river and because it was a moment to treasure, I started to hum one of the themes of Beethoven's *Symphonie Pastorale.* There was no going back.

We all loved music. G. was a miner's son from the north of England. He didn't want to work in a mine for the rest of his life so he went to night school and eventually became a metallurgist engineer. He also discovered that he loved music and taught himself to play the trumpet. That day, G., C. and I started our own symphony orchestra ... singing parts of the symphonies, concertos and the classics that we loved.

A. was a specialist in English songs of three kinds: pub songs, sailor songs, and rugby songs. These were more difficult to learn, but they sure enriched my vocabulary!

On the 23rd, our third day in Srinagar, we went to Gulmarg, which was a lovely valley to the north of Srinagar. The British used to play polo there. The floor of the valley is a huge green saucer surrounded by pine forest. We could see the cottages built by the expats who had been anxious to leave the heat of the plains for the coolness of Kashmir.

We got horses and rode all over the valley, with those glorious mountain peaks surrounding us.

On the 25th we went to Pahalgam, a small village from where we would begin a five-day trek into the mountains further north. With pack ponies to carry our tents, bedding, etc., we formed a small caravan, led by Abdul and some of his male relatives (I think!)

The next day we made our first stop for lunch in a small hamlet called Aru, on our way to Lidderwat. Our lunch menu did not vary much once we were on the road: kebabs, boiled eggs and cold baked potatoes (these at every meal).

We were now on ponies all the time. My own horse was called LaLa. As luck would have it, she was the leader of the pack. With only the sky before me, a cliff on one side, and a precipice on the other, I was glad LaLa was sure-footed.

One of Abdul's relatives walked beside me—but if the mountain gods had been in the mood for a sacrifice, they could have easily taken all three of us. We made camp in a valley on the way to the Kolahoi Glacier ... talk about wilderness! Our caravan helpers smoked their water pipes (I hope nothing else!) and we played a game of dice after dinner on improvised tables and chairs. Then, it was bed for us, in our blue tent of Australian fame!

The next day, the 27th, we left at 5 a.m. for the Kolahoi Glacier (after tea of course!) On the way, we had to cross many small creeks. It had to be done in the morning, before the snow melted upstream and they got too fast and high. We reached one swollen creek that Abdul deemed too dangerous for C. and I to cross, so we were left behind and got a well-deserved rest … in advance!

On the 28th, we were glad of our early rest, because we went climbing again. Our goal this time was the Yemher pass (13,400 feet). It was very high—too high for anyone with any sense to climb in the conditions under which we did).

Crossing a narrow icefield (almost on all four!) G. lost his footing slightly and would have fallen a good few hundred feet, and right before my eyes! That day the mountain gods must have been looking somewhere else.

None of us were prepared for the trek we had embarked on. G. was wearing running shoes, and A. was in a pair of good sandals as were C. and I. And here we were crossing glaciers almost crawling!

Near the top of the pass, C. gave up. By the time I had made sure she was okay (one of the "relatives" was with her) the group had gone ahead, so I climbed after them and reached the top just in time to join them behind our respective rocks to be sick. No wonder! We were at about 13,500 feet, level with dozens of peaks all around which, like the last part of the pass, were covered with snow. Being thirsty, I had eaten some—not very bright of me, as all climbers know.

How Not to Climb is a book that the four of us could have written. We had no walking sticks, no oxygen, no good shoes, and no warm clothes. I wore jeans and my ever-present cotton plaid blouse.

On the way down, my legs were like rags. LaLa knew the way home, and picked her way daintily down the mountainside. Me

… I was holding Abdul's hand. I could hardly walk!

Going back to Pahalgam the next day, we stopped again in Aru. We met groups of nomadic families. The women were laden with heavy jewellery, and the ponies with children, pots, pans, carpets, and tents. We saw more little mountain ponies, relatives of my friend LaLa. I can't thank her enough for getting me home safely.

When we got back to Pahalgam, we took a car to Srinagar, and our home on the lake. No shikara for us that night, just a long relaxed talk on our roof terrace. The lake was so still….

On our last day together, we went for a picnic (cold baked potatoes included) at the Shalimar Gardens near Srinagar.

We went to Kashmir for the cooler climate of course, but also because of a song that C. loved. I have to quote it as a tribute to one of the loveliest places on the planet.

(At the time I didn't know who wrote it or to whom it refers, but I have since learned that it is an Edwardian love song composed by Laurence Hope and Amy Woodforde-Finden, and inspired by time spent in India.)

Kashmiri Song

Pale hands I loved beside the Shalimar,
Where are you now? Who lies beneath your spell?
Whom do you lead on Rapture's roadway, far,
Before you agonize them in farewell?

Pale hands, pink-tipped, like lotus buds that float
On those cool waters where we used to dwell,
I would have rather felt you round my throat,
Crushing out life, than waving me farewell!

Pale hands I loved beside the Shalimar,
Where are you now? Where are you now?
Pale hands, pink-tipped, like lotus buds that float
On those cool waters where we used to dwell,

I would have rather felt you round my throat
Crushing out life, than waving me farewell!
Pale hands I loved beside the Shalimar,
Where are you now? Where are you now?

It was time for us to say farewell, as G. and A. had to go back to work. C. and I could certainly not afford to stay on the Highland Queen on our own, so after their departure, it was camping in Pahalgam for us. We had shared many interesting, scary, musical, wonderful moments with those two and had become very close. Of course, they had paid for most of what we did and that was upsetting for us. But, gentlemen that they were, they made us feel that it had been the most fun, pleasant and enjoyable leave they had ever had. Amen.

Chapter 14

India and South Ceylon

18 June, 1956   *Bombay*

I thought we would stay in India for three weeks and I
am still here after a month and a half. We left Srinagar on
the 10th of June. On the 11th, we went to Amritsar (near
the border of Pakistan) to see the Golden Temple of the
Sikh religion. That same night we were on the train for
Delhi. We left Delhi right away, so I can't say that I have
seen much of the capital of India! I was sorry about that,
especially when I learned that our ship is not leaving on
the 15th of July as planned, but on the 22nd!

We were disappointed, but we have decided to travel
south by land to get on board the MV Isipingo in Colombo. The ship will get us to Durban, South Africa by
the end of July. After that, we will make no more trips
for a few months as we have been on the move since the

27th of January.

I can't claim to know India, but I have seen a lot of it. They say that the south is more interesting than the north. I sent you a little souvenir of Kashmir. Did you get it? Gifts for you don't rain anymore like they did from Japan! I don't get anything from the Canadian government anymore! Poor, poor me.

In Bombay we are staying at the Salvation Army Hostel. It is right near the port and in front of the Taj Mahal Hotel, which is one of the best in India. We go there a lot. Though we may sleep like paupers, we spend the days in great luxury. Nobody questions us!

On our way to Bombay, we spent a day in Agra visiting the Taj Mahal. I didn't see it under a full moon, but it was a marvel as is the Red Fort, built circa 1526 by the Mogul emperor of the time. I saw the harem, the emperor's apartments, as well as those of the princes and princesses. They knew what luxury was! For years, 2,000 workers were constructing the Taj Mahal. I don't like to think how many died.

We are going back to Calcutta now (two days on the train....)

It turned out to be nearly three. We slept in our seats. In the third class women's compartment of the train, we shared what little food we had with the women travellers, and they shared with us. They mended C.'s skirts and made room for us among all the baggage and kids they had with them. The men travelled in lonely third class splendour in a different compartment of the train. All of the third class compartments had wooden seats and barred windows.

The trains in India, which we got to know so well, were old, not too clean, and a bit (or a lot!) in need of maintenance. But they did work well. It was a lifeline in a poor country with few good roads. People like us could go anywhere for just a few annas (pennies). Except for one or two times, we chose to travel in third class, in the women's compartment whenever it was possible.

I had gone to India with stars in my eyes. I had read a wonderful book called *Le Pèlerinage aux Sources* by Lanza del Vasto, which described a soul-searching voyage through the subcontinent by a philosopher in need of fulfilment. The reality of the country hit me like a ton of bricks.

I had never seen such misery and poverty. There were mutilated children in the arms of beggars at each train stop, crippled adults, and the sad, sad eyes of the women. I will never forget a little boy beating his hands against his swollen tummy to make a "tom-tom" sound in order to get annas.

Because we were Westerners, we were in a caste apart, and at that moment in time, considered superior. The other Western travellers we chanced to meet looked at us in horror because of the way we were travelling. If I have a good memory of India, it is of the beauty of the country and all those poor women we met in third class. They were beautiful, generous, and found it in their souls to laugh, wipe their kids' noses with their amazing saris, and look after us too.

3 July, 1956   *Chitaldrug*

To my great surprise, I find myself in the south of India. Our ship, which was supposed to leave Calcutta on the 8th of June, then on the 30th, will finally leave on the

28th of July! We have decided to join the ship in Colombo and that way we can see the south of India and Ceylon.

The girls we visited were working for a U.S. religious society. They had a small infirmary, but since they were not nurses they did only basic work. Their main task was to convert people, as missionaries do. So once a week, they would put on their saris and go down to a nearby village in their old black car.

They asked us to join them one day, and we dutifully put on saris and sailed forth to observe. As good Catholics, we couldn't do much more! They stood on the corner of two paths amidst a few poor huts and started to read the Bible in loud voices. Then we went to visit a family. Our duty done, we got in the car to go home, but it did not want to start! It is something for me, in my old age, to laugh about: three sari-clad Western girls, very clumsy in these long garments, pushing a car and driver towards our hill. Mon Dieu!

They were very generous and fed us well. We paid them something for our room and board, of course, but they had cupboards full of food, so I'm sure they didn't starve after our departure.

16 July, 1956   *Kandy (Ceylon)*

I haven't written for a while, so I will try to fill you in on the events that led me to Kandy.

After our return to Calcutta on the 21st of June, we went to Madras. There I saw the church where the martyred body of St. Thomas rests.

After that, we took the train again to Bangalore, then carried on by bus to our destination: the small village of Chitaldrug. We spent a week there with the U.S. missionary girls that we had met in Kashmir. C. was not feeling well. We were supposed to stay only for two days but instead we spent a week resting. When C. was in better health, we went to Cochin, Trivandrum and Cape Comorin (at the tip of India). Then we took the train to Madurai and a boat to Ceylon, where I am now.

Imagine my surprise to find that in India there is a city called Trivandrum, where you find a majority of Catholics! There were churches everywhere. They are full on Sunday and everywhere there are nuns and priests in white cassocks. On the street, people wear medals around their necks and there are pictures of the Holy Family above the doors of many houses. The apostle St. Thomas was the first to arrive in Trivandrum, followed by St. Francis Xavier. The people here are older Catholics than we are! It was a pleasure to see that, especially after visiting temples where they worship cows and stone gods.

When we were south of Cochin in Trivandrum, we took a day trip from Ernakulam to Alleppey. We had to choose between taking the bus, or taking the boat down the backwaters (a sort of canal). We decided to take the boat. It was a wonderful change. The canal was narrow and surrounded on either side with banks of tropical vegetation. There were lovely villages here and there full of children who were enjoying the water. They were fishing from the shore using huge nets on poles.

The little boat, which was a bit like a small barge with seats, had a surprise for us. At the back of the boat, on a platform, were two enclosures with walls reaching only to the waist. It was the best scenic toilet in the world. You didn't have to miss a single palm tree! Someone (not me, thank you) could write a book about the "basic facilities" I have seen in my travels, need I say more!

Back in Colombo, our ship had been delayed once again. Such was the price you had to pay to travel cheap by freighters. They had no room for us at the Y in Colombo. We had to sleep in their games room, so they suggested we go to Kandy.

We arrived in Kandy at dusk, and were walking to our accommodation when we heard the ringing of bells. In a few minutes, we came face to face with an elephant on his way home! My, they are big. In Kandy, our rooming house was run by an old woman. She was descended from Dutch settlers who called themselves Burghers. They were a small, elite group. She was very kind and gave us a few lifts to places of interest around town in an old car. It was always the same ritual. She would start the car with lots of clutch pumping, and then let her chauffeur drive!

On the 20th of July we were back at the Colombo Y where they had beds for us—and on the 21st the Isipingo arrived! Finally on the 30th, we went aboard to be greeted by a stewardess! Incredible! We had tea with the captain, an occurrence that can be explained by the fact that there were very few people on board! We left on the 31st.

16 July, 1956   *MV Isipingo*

To think that in a month I will be in South Africa. Our ship goes directly to Durban from Colombo. I don't know how long we will stay in Africa. Probably a year. We have exhausted our reserves and since we want to see Africa, the Middle East and Europe, we will need to save some money.

It seems a long time and I am more homesick than a year ago. On the other hand, this is what I want to do and I am very happy.

Chapter 15

MV Isipingo

31 July - 12 August, 1956

We finally left Colombo on the 31st of July, on the MV Isipingo. It was a ship like the Changsha, with freight and passengers. We were in second class, of course. There were so few passengers that, with a new friend we made in first class, and a very friendly captain and officers, we were free to enjoy most facilities.

It was really a trip "sans histoire", with not much happening. We played deck tennis, chess, and darts, we had drinks and informal parties, but nothing was organized because there were so few of us.

We never realized until we got to South Africa what a colour bar meant. Apartheid was not fully implemented when we arrived, but it may as well have been. It was one of the reasons there was such little passenger traffic between India and South Africa.

The ship didn't stop anywhere. We passed the island of Mayotte, in the Comoros, and we saw the coast of Mozambique. We arrived in Durban on the 12th of August, at night. It was a wonderful sight from our ship.

At this point, it is interesting to compare the three ships on which I had travelled thus far. The MV Changsha, named after a seaport and the capital of Hunan province in China, was built in 1949 in Scotland. Its gross tonnage was 7,412 tons. Gross tonnage is a measure of the internal capacity of a ship. It is a space measurement of all areas of a vessel with some allowances or deductions for exempt spaces such as living quarters. The officers were British and the crew was Chinese. There were seventy passengers aboard.

The Changsha was great fun. We had parties (all seventy of us!) The passengers were mostly Australians, which accounted for the good atmosphere on board. We were all equal. Only the price and location of cabins was different. The officers were great guys.

Our little MV Sibigo was also built in 1949, but in Holland. It was named after a town on Simeulue Island, west of Aceh province in Indonesia. It had room for eight passengers, and was 2,185 tons … almost the same tonnage as a submarine! The officers were Dutch and the crew Indonesian. Of the Sibigo, what can I say? I loved it the most. It was comfortable, like a home on the sea, shared by new and very good friends. We stopped at many little out-of-the-way ports.

It was a different story on the MV Santhia, the worst of the lot. It was not very clean, and the class barrier was strictly enforced. There were no more smiling officers. We must have had a captain, but we never saw him in second class! The food was poor and monotonous. To this day, I can't stand plum pudding!

The MV Santhia was named after a district in India, now known as Bangladesh. It was built in Scotland, and was 8,907 tons. It was divided into first class, cabin class (us of course) and steerage. The officers were English and the crew was Indian.

The MV Isipingo was the ship that took us to Africa from India. It was the most luxurious of them all. It was 7,073 tons, and was built in Belfast in 1934. It was named after a coastal area north of Durban, and a river too, if I remember well. There was accommodation for fifty people in first class, and a few more than that in second class. There were so few passengers on our own trip that these numbers were irrelevant.

The Isipingo was great, if very quiet. They were gracious enough to let us stay on board while we fought with Customs in Durban for our entrance to the country. I remember them as a marvellous shipping company with the best captain. At the time, the Isipingo was renowned as a top-of-the-line ship, but I can't remember the "great rooms" at all. In the back of my mind, I seem to recall some of them were closed off. The British ship officers were very friendly, as was the captain. To our great relief, the food was good.

Chapter 16

Durban, South Africa

21 August, 1956   *Durban*

After a lot of adventures, we have finally disembarked
in South Africa. Because we had to wait almost a month
in India before sailing, both C. and I had to spend some
of our famous 100 pounds required for entry in the
country.

I can't tell you much about this place yet. It is very
strange to see signs at bus stops stating "for Europeans
only" and benches on the sidewalks that are "for Europeans only." One would think that black people didn't
exist. You meet them out on the street, but that is all.
They look happy and the ones unloading the ships are
singing all the time.

Among the black people I saw in town, there was not
a single teenager. It was as if they went straight from be-

ing carried on their mother's back to adulthood!

Durban is a modern city and is very clean. It has nothing to do with the jungle.

We are looking for work and for a flat. Since the day we got here, it has been a constant battle with Immigration.

We arrived in Durban on the 12th of August and finally left the ship yesterday (the 20th) after trying as hard as we could to get into the country. I have never felt so unwanted in my life.

As I said before, we didn't have the required 100 pounds each for entrance to the country so we needed a job or a sponsor.

We tried to find a sponsor first, at the suggestion of the Customs' officers. They directed us to a club that had been formed especially to help English immigrants. It was called the 1820 Settlers Association. I don't remember what 1820 meant but I remember very well Colonel H., who was its director. We went there many times without success. They even wanted more money from us than Customs required.

Then we contacted a Canadian Women's Club. After one look at us wanderers, especially the "French one" we left empty-handed, after tea ... bien sûr!

A kind parishioner of our local Oblate Father saved us. This kind man was the owner of a mattress factory. We never met him. Bless his heart and soul.

We were looking for jobs at the same time, of course. But it was a difficult task to go about when we didn't know anyone or anything about the place and were not sure of ever landing as legitimate citizens! We soon found out that social work was out of the question. We

didn't speak Afrikaans (African Dutch). We tried department stores, and went to the big companies like Shell
and Lever Bros. ... but had no luck.

The whole time we were battling with Immigration we were
able to stay aboard the Isipingo. I wonder what would have
happened to us if the ship had needed to leave? Would they
have kept us as crew? Doing what? Cooking?

31 August, 1956   *Durban*

I am sending you my new address. We expect to be
here until Christmas. Our flat is in a concrete block of
flats. We have a kitchen, a bathroom, a bedroom, a living
room and a dining room. Furniture is more than scarce
but we manage. We are going to ask for some apple boxes to make small tables. We could have had a small flat
but ... living together is not always easy for C. and I. We
are very different and we both have different faults. But
it could be worse.

Durban is mostly English, making it easier (in a manner
of speaking) for us to find work. The Afrikaans-speak-
ing South Africans are the descendants of the Boers.
They don't like English people, and now that they have
political power, they want to make everyone learn and
speak Afrikaans. It is a good idea, but not for the two of
us. Thank God for that accent of mine. Do you realize
that I speak English almost all of the time now? Except
with C., I read in English and see English films.

Good news! I have found work at the Municipal Library of Durban. It is a good job.

All is well now after the problems we had when we first arrived. C. has found a job at Dunlop and we have good salaries—enough to live on and save too. We will try to find better if possible.

Our apartment is a little jewel. We have our souvenirs on display here and there: pewter plates and teak elephants from Malaya.

I sent you some little carpets made of wool from Kashmir. Did you get them?

The few black people I see I cannot speak to. They have special places. Or it might be more accurate to say no place instead, because everything seems to be reserved for Europeans!

Last Sunday we went to see some Zulu dancers. What rhythm, and the way they dress! Feathers, animal skins, beads and amazing colours! It has been our only outing so far.

I like my work at the library. I meet all kinds of people, polite, rude, interesting, dull....

At Dunlop C. got a job as a dispatch clerk. She was later promoted to the pay office but she was quite lost with pounds, shillings and pence! Give me the library's Dewey Decimal System any day. As for me, I was desperately looking for work. I saw that the main library in the Municipal Hall needed librarians! I love to read and figured that qualified me. They thought the same, fortunately, and after interviews, an appearance in front of a panel and a medical check-up, I was hired! Of course, I fully intended to make it a life career and take some courses to learn more about my job! Not really a lie … I might have never left Durban, who is to say! In fact I nearly didn't….

I could write a book of advice on how to get (or not get) a job in a foreign country … if you manage to get into the country, that is!

9 December, 1956   *Durban*

It is a bit difficult to give you an idea of what I do here. When we arrived in Durban, we had great difficulty landing, as you know. But we have been lucky. I love my work, which is not very tiring. I take in books, give back cards, and print the date on the books taken out. It is a surprise for me to see how many people think that I come from Scotland or Ireland. I learned to speak English from all kinds of people with all kinds of different accents. Everyone is surprised to know that I come from Canada, of which I am very proud.

I work from 8 a.m. until 4 p.m. or 12 p.m. to 8 p.m. I prefer the evening shift because I can go to the beach and swim in the big pool there. I can also go into the sea. The surf is marvellous; the waves are quite high, even better than in Australia. I am not very brave but it is great to be near the ocean.

If we want to go to Europe when we leave, we will need some more money.

We have not seen much of South Africa so far. First, we had to get settled, find work and a flat. We will soon begin hitchhiking again. We have found that it is a great way to see a country. I must admit that it will be more risky with all these black people who complain of their treatment by white people (and are right to.) Soon, the country will be partitioned in two, with a big part for the whites I expect. Maybe it will be better to separate all the black people than to humiliate them as is done now. At the library, they were not allowed in unless sent by their "missus," and even then, they have to use a side door! I don't have a chance to get to know them, since I am always with Europeans.

17 December, 1956   *Durban*

We intend to move to Johannesburg at the end of January. The salaries are better even if life is quite different. There are lots of black people there.

Don't send letters by boat anymore. They take at least a month and a half to arrive.

We want to go to Basutoland (Lesotho) for the New Year. We have been invited by Father G., an Oblate Father we met in our parish. I didn't get a holiday for Christmas and I am anxious to meet some French Canadians.

I am taking typing lessons at a typing school in the evenings after work, in case I can't find social work in Johannesburg.

This letter will arrive just a few days before Christmas. You know that I think about you all the time. Merry Christmas!

10 January, 1957   *Durban*

I am back in South Africa. I can't tell you how much I enjoyed the New Year in Basutoland.

We left by train on the 28th of December for Ficksburg (Orange Free State). We met a nice family who brought us to St. Monique, which is Father G.'s mission. He put us up in the rooms reserved for visiting priests. On Sunday, we went to Mass. Hearing the *Gloria in Excelsis Deo* in the local language was very strange! After that, we went touring around some villages. You should have seen us among all these little black kids who wore nothing but medals!

On Monday, we went to the centre of Basutoland to an old mission of Father G.'s. We stopped in Roma where they are building a university. The fathers and the nuns there gave us some maple syrup and I cried like a baby. Everyone we have met has treated us like family. They are real darlings.

I told Father G. that you always sent money to the missions. He looked in his files and there you were—a faithful contributor.

We left on the 2nd of February and had to hitchhike back here because the train was late.

7 February, 1957   *Durban*

I haven't made up my mind about South Africa yet. After I have been here a while, I think I'll have a better feel for it. Coming from a country without these kinds of problems, it is easy to criticize.

There is a black guy who looks after our flat—he cleans and polishes the floors. If he did our wash I would think myself back in Japan, spoiled child that I am!

If I were asked to settle in South Africa I would say no. I would have to choose between ignoring what is going on or acting on the black people's behalf. Because I am a coward, I don't know that I could do so, and I love my beautiful Canada. Luckily, it is not a choice I have to make.

Beside working and swimming, I cook. That is, we cook. The first one home prepares the meal. Tonight, it is Canadian salmon—a real treat. It is terribly expensive here, as is chicken. I won't complain. We eat very well, and have enough fruit to make us sick! Today is Friday and Friday is market day. We go to shop at the market every week with some neighbours who have a car. This is what I bought today: 2 pineapples, 8 apples (expensive), 2 peaches, 4 pears, grapes, 12 bananas, potatoes, carrots, corn, tomatoes, lettuce, cabbage, onions and a cucumber. Not bad if you think that the whole lot cost ten shillings, which is about one dollar. We eat mostly salads at the moment because it is so hot!

We don't know many people in Durban yet. My working colleagues are very nice but seem much younger than me. A few are Catholics, but Catholicism is not too popular. The Afrikaners of the Dutch Reformed Church are very strict. If you ask me what I think of them, it will not be too flattering. I like the English South Africans one hundred percent better. They are more tolerant. Did you know television is not allowed in the country?

Our first few months in Durban were very quiet. We went to Johannesburg for a weekend and we also went with two English guys from our block of flats for the weekend to a national park with the impossible name of Hluhluwe. Without the Zulu click diphthong you can't really pronounce it.

There, we saw zebras and wildebeest. In fact, one of them stared at us so much that we made a hasty retreat. There was only one tree on that plain—and the guys had it! Cowards!

We had to find some basic furniture for our flat. The search for a cheap stove lasted quite a while. In the meantime someone lent us a small oven that we put on two chairs. Our cakes, our most favourite food, always came out of it looking like ski slopes—thick at one end and thin at the other!

We were not sure if we would stay in Durban. All we wanted was money to see Africa and Europe. One day we saw the answer to our prayers in the newspaper. Peter Townsend, the ex-boyfriend of Princess Margaret, was going on a safari crossing the whole continent, from Cape Town to North Africa. He needed to assemble a crew for his trip. We wrote offering our services … as cooks! Of course we never even got a reply. So much for our gourmet efforts! They did not miss much.

While we were pursuing that dream balloon, we got the most marvellous gift in the world. On loan from a colleague of C. we got … yes, a beautiful sewing machine! It was a table model without electricity or pedals. The needles had to be moved by hand using a big wheel, so you turned the wheel with your right hand while sewing with your left. It was no mean feat, but for us, having sewn skirts and sundresses by hand, it was a dream come true.

When I read my diary and letters from the last four years of our odyssey I wonder who in the world would have had the courage to appear in public with us! We spent next to nothing on clothes, we had so few, and they were well worn-out before we spent our precious pennies on replacing them. We made curtains and bedspreads on our little sewing machine. The two of us worked together when it got too difficult for just one person to keep the seam straight. We always used the cheapest material as well!

My own work of art was a pink dress made from cheap curtain material in a sort of jacquard. It had a round neck and reached just below the knee. It was also a good fit. But unfortunately, nobody told me that with this kind of cloth I had to finish the seams! It took no time at all for the cut edges to loosen up. Inside out it looked as if I was wearing a fringe dress! It looked good while it lasted. I think about it with fond memories.

By January of 1957, it was clear that we either had to stay in Durban or move again to start looking for jobs and flats in Johannesburg. We had received no answer to our applications so we decided to stay. We moved to a flat near the sea—it was small but new, and a block from the beach, hotels and the swimming pool. C. had joined a badminton club and I started to go to some youth hostel meetings in view of our planned trip to Europe through Africa.

19 March, 1957   Durban

Many things have happened since my last letter. I told you we had applied for jobs in Johannesburg. They answered us too late. Our apartment was too expensive so we have moved and decided to stay here in Durban.

Our new flat is very nice. We are near the beach this time and a few minutes from the port. We can swim all year around here and the sea is so beautiful. Since we are very thrifty we have made curtains and bedspreads with some cotton ticking material from Dunlop that we purchased for a few shillings. All we need now is a few chairs. At the moment we have cushions on the floor.

We live near a church where there is a French-Canadian priest. On Wednesdays, at his request, we go to the church for the Sailors' Club dances. It is very nice. We dance in front of a statue of the Virgin Mary! I meet all kinds of people. Sometimes they are French-speaking and are delighted to speak to C. and I.

I have also found another job that I work at during the day when I am not at the library. I start at noon and am a sort of secretary for a geography professor at the university!

I am looking out at the sea. It is high tide. The surf is also high. It is so beautiful. Father G. just brought us some maple syrup. He lets us use the rectory fridge to keep our meat cold. A great help.

Our social life was also getting better. At a youth hostel meeting I met B., a Jewish young man who became a great friend. He took me to his synagogue a few times on Fridays. I loved the service music and was quite intrigued by the segregation of men and women—and the lack of attention and gossip going on up there among the ladies! B.'s father had an ostrich farm that was fun to visit. I even went to a wedding with him. There was lots of music, dance and good food.

And then, at the youth hostel meeting in March, I met K., a very nice English engineer. We talked about our lives in South Africa, Canada, and England, and agreed to meet again. That first evening he came to get me after work, it was pouring rain. We had to run to get to his car, which was a fair distance from the building. I thought it was great fun running in the rain….

Later he told me it was then that he fell in love with me—that girl from Québec. We went out a lot. My work schedule was not regular and he lived in bachelor quarters near his own work, in a little town that was a good twenty miles from me so it was a feat for us to see each other at all!

He had a sort of "bathtub car" where only our heads were showing. It was some sort of English Morris I think. Later, after going to England for three months, he came back with a blue Volkswagen … a big improvement.

Shortly after we started going out together, he invited me to a party at his prestigious company club.

When we arrived, the members were having sundowners on the veranda. They were all very smart and polished, and looked at me in a state of shock. Here was their most eligible bachelor … spoken for!

I had my new pink dress (before it frayed apart), but all the same I felt like a zoo animal. I was new to this very colonial "Englishness" of the expatriates. We were to encounter more of this later on in Rhodesia.

19 May, 1957   *Durban*

Durban has an ideal climate. We take turns sleeping on the balcony because we only have room for one bed inside. Since the rain comes from the west and we face east, all is well.

At work, I have been having problems with my legs because I must stand all the time. I asked to go to another department. Cataloguing would be best, as I would not have to stand.

21 *August, 1957*   ***Durban***

We will have two weeks of holiday starting on the 29th of August. We will first go to Kruger National Park where one can see a lot of wild animals. Lions and elephants are free to roam. People must stay in their cars or camps. It is a sort of zoo in reverse. Then we will go back to Johannesburg and travel south to Cape Town. We will come back on the East Coast all the way to Durban.

One of the girls at the library has influenza. There is an epidemic here.

4 *September, 1957*   ***near Cape Town***

It seems incredible but it is true. I am writing to you from the porch of the farm of Meneer D.T. where we have been staying since yesterday. He is an Afrikaner. As you probably know, the Dutch, French, and German Huguenots were among the first Europeans to come to South Africa (meeting the black tribes halfway) to form the Afrikaner people. The Afrikaners don't want to speak English and certainly don't speak French anymore.

While hitchhiking from Johannesburg to Cape Town, a young man gave us a lift and invited us to stay on his family farm for a few days. It was a marvellous opportunity for us. The farm is situated at the foot of a mountain and it dominates the valley where wheat, grapes and all kinds of vegetables grow very well. The house is about 150 years old.

The walls are very thick, like the ones at the house of the aunts at l'Île d'Orléans. They are whitewashed and covered with bougainvillaea. There is no electricity. I would like to spend more time here, but we must leave for Cape Town tomorrow. We will return to Durban by the Garden Route on the east coast because of all the wildflowers blooming right now. The rainy season is over and I hope we will have nice weather. There are vineyards everywhere around here. There are no Zulus or Basutos, but many Hottentots, a very different people. Back on the 16th?

We made two long trips while in Durban, one to the north and one to the south, hitchhiking all the way. On our first sightseeing tour, we left Durban for Johannesburg where we stayed in a very dirty youth hostel. Then we were off to Sabie and Pretoria, the capital. We wanted to see the town, so we joined a tour bus. Most of the passengers were Afrikaners. The driver/guide was bilingual. I don't think he heard us speak French between ourselves but he certainly heard us speak English. So, while we stood on a hill looking at Pretoria, the driver, staring at us both, started to give a speech pointing out all the grievances that the Afrikaners had with England. It was a bit like the speeches at our "Patriotic Days" when I was young. Now, this was different. To him, we were English! What a turn. We put him right. I was not pleased by the attack, but "c'est la vie."

We reached Bloemfontein on the 3rd and on the 4th we stopped at the farm mentioned in my letter. I thought it was paradise with its huge fields of sweet peas, ripe and so good.

What was not so nice was the way this farmer treated his black workers. Before sundown, he would put one cup of wine dregs on the shed floor and call his "boys" in for a drink. Mevrouw, the mother, didn't want her son to make friends with us. We were adventuresses of the worst kind!

The city of Cape Town was lovely though, and we stayed at the Y. It was a beautiful trip back to Durban through fields of wildflowers. We passed through an area called the Transkei, where orange-brown was the colour of choice for the natives' clothing, with sort of a Nefertiti hairstyle worn by the women.

We got home on the 14th. Our flat was full of flowers from K., my engineer friend! It had been Guy Fawkes Night on the 5th of November. I had never heard of the guy! It was not taught in my school. We had a big party at K.'s club. Between trips, we went to Zululand and the Drakensberg Mountains also. The "bathtub" was a car after all and could get us places!

November 1957   *Durban*

These are our plans for next year. We will stay two weeks in Basutoland. From there we will go to Lourenço Marques and Mombasa on the east coast. We will then cross to the west coast of Africa. We will take a boat that goes on the Congo River to Pointe-Noire. There, we will catch a French ship going to Bordeaux, stopping here and there on the west coast of France.

NB. We had first planned to go to Egypt by road or train but our plans have been upset by the Suez Canal crisis.

I am anxious and not anxious to go at the same time. It will not be easy to cross and leave Africa since we now have a lot of friends.

I have just enough money to reach England. After that, I will have to borrow some for my passage home, otherwise you will never see me again! I will talk about it later.

In a few weeks, it will be Christmas. I will buy your gifts this week. While you are getting ready to freeze, here it is hot.

I bought seven roses for one shilling at the market and a chrysanthemum for half a shilling. We always have flowers in the flat.

Christmas, 1958   *Durban*

No more Congo. The latest news is that our ship to France from there will cost twice the original price. We have decided to change our plans. We will stay here until the end of January, travel in Africa in February and leave on the 7th of March on an Italian ship for Europe. We have had a crazy week while reorganizing the whole thing.

For Christmas we had a paper tree that was one and a half feet high.

C. and I invited K. and a Frenchman for Midnight Mass and a "réveillon." K., who is a Protestant, does not get on his knees very often, but I told him that a bit of humility is good for him!

The next day, I had Christmas dinner (lunch) at the staff house where K. works. His parents are in London, and we are two orphans. To celebrate the New Year, I went to a dance at the club where he works. I stayed with friends and the next morning we went to the beach nearby.

Here I am, writing to you from Rhodesia. Let me bring you up to date with our travels since my last letter. On the 1ˢᵗ of February we left Durban to go north, our longest trip since we had gone south to Cape Town earlier. We returned to Johannesburg on the 23ʳᵈ and went to Maseru (Basutoland). We were back in Durban at the beginning of March.

When we left, we went through Johannesburg again and Pretoria. On the 2ⁿᵈ, it was Pietersburg and Messina. We had no problems on the road ... so far. We reached the frontier of South Rhodesia on the 3ʳᵈ and stayed the night in Bulawayo. Most of our lifts were with families. We stayed with one of them for the night.

The next day we were at the Victoria Falls; it was a marvellous sight. We could go as near to the falls as our courage would allow us. It was great to feel the gentle spray of water and hear the roar of the water. We couldn't afford a meal at the posh Victoria Falls Hotel, but we had a drink.

On the 6ᵗʰ we were on our way to Lusaka, a town that we had trouble getting out of. We had to wait five hours on the road just outside town. Finally we got a ride ("it only takes one" was our mantra) for Petauke and its rest house. The next day we were on to Fort Jameson, where we planned to visit a mission staffed by French Canadians.

The good Father saying his prayers on the porch nearly fell off his rocking chair when he saw those two wanderers from Québec. In those days, you left for the missions for life—but that day home came to him.

If you could see me right now you would be jealous. I am in a corner of paradise called the mission of St. Anne at Fort Jameson, in the north of Rhodesia. We wanted to go to the Congo but it is the rainy season here and we didn't want to get stuck in the north.

You can imagine the surprise of F. when she saw me. (F. is a former Girl Guide leader from Québec. She became a nun, and certainly didn't ever expect to see me in Africa!)

Since we've been here, I have not stopped talking. This morning we visited a local native village. There are four white Fathers here who are very nice. Not many French Canadians come visiting this way, especially not hitchhikers. They are feeding us like princesses. We eat mangos, papayas and avocados.

After our stay at Fort Jameson, we wanted to go across Lake Nyasa (Malawi). We got to the boat by train from Salima. It was called the Ilala and was a sort of freight train on the water that stopped here and there to deliver goods. On board were six passengers: two English civil servants, their wives and us. More expats with pretentious accents, according to C.

At Nkhotakota, we had a party on board! It was great fun! In the morning we visited a mission in Nkhata Bay.

On board, all the passengers were gossiping about a Scottish man who was living with a black woman. He had come to a landing somewhere to get supplies and stayed on with her. They were scandalized. According to them he was letting the Empire down!

Like its name indicates, Lake Nyasa was mostly in Nyasaland, but before we reached our destination of Malawi, we had already been in the Tanzanian part of the lake for a day.

The Customs officer gave us a lift to Katumbi, then we visited a district commissioner's headquarters at Karonga with him. One of the commissioner's assistants had been a student at Oxford University. He was lonely, homesick and glad of some company. We spent the night at the guesthouse at headquarters. The next day, our Customs officer gave us a lift to Mbeya. There we went to a small hotel. It was cold as we were at 5,000 feet!

We were hoping to cross to Rhodesia the next day but we got there too late! The Customs officers (who could have let us go) were very friendly. Amazingly enough there was an American couple also stranded with us. We had drinks all around and our friends opened the border the next day … right on time.

After a few more days of adventures, we made Lusaka, Harare, Chegutu, and finally Gweru on the 19th. On our way to the Zimbabwe ruins, we had the worst lift of our life. The roads were flooded (we got back just before they were closed) and there was little traffic. The three guys who stopped for us had been drinking—they were amusing themselves by talking about hitting monkeys. Naïve as we were, we thought they meant animals! But no, they were looking for black people to run down. They were not good advertising for white Rhodesians.

The Zimbabwe ruins were great and unexpectedly big. There were only two other people looking around them. There was no guide, no rules and no entry fee. We thought it was a shame that such a treasure was so neglected.

In Gweru, we were lucky enough to get a ride all the way to Johannesburg. The road was terrible, only two-wheel tracks most of the time. One enterprising farmer's wife had set a canvas shelter by the road and was serving tea! We bought some while admiring a group of giraffes munching their lunch up in the sky! This trip finished up in Maseru, Basutoland, for a short visit. Then it was farewell to Durban.

4 March, 1958   *Durban*

A short note done in haste since we are leaving tomorrow. K. is picking me up in an hour so I can go around saying goodbye. It is harder to leave this time, as we have stayed here longer than we did in Australia.

I think that I will arrive in London with five dollars in my pocket! I get off in Venice, Italy, on the 24th of March. We will stay three days and then go straight to London. I hope to return to the continent!

5 March, 1958   *Durban*

I leave at noon. Everything is ready. It is 8:30 a.m. I am still in pyjamas.

Chapter 17

MV Africa, Lloyd Triestino
11,427 tons, 346 passengers

We left Durban in the afternoon after sad farewells. K. and I had decided that I would be back in a few months.

I had written home about my plans to marry an Englishman who happened to be Protestant at the same time! My family was shocked of course, and a bit hurt. They suggested I come home for a while before I made up my mind.

It would have been very hard to let C. go to Europe alone to finish our trip. The whole point of the exercise had been to have enough money to see Europe while getting a glimpse of some other parts of the world. I couldn't let her down, and I needed to go back to base. C. got sick in London and it was a good thing we stayed together after all.

Well—I was on my way to Europe, finally. Our ship, a passenger one, was Italian. We first stopped in Beira, then in Dar es Salaam. We had to go ashore by shuttle boat, as we could not dock. We took a bus to Oyster Bay. We also stopped in Zanzibar, which had such a romantic and faraway-sounding name.

In Mombasa, we saw Fort Jesus (I believe that is what it was called!) where they kept the slaves waiting for "shipment." There is no other word for the way they were treated. We had a day there, so we made the most of it. It was a lovely colonial-style town.

On the 13th we reached Mogadishu, Somalia, where we picked up Italian soldiers who were stationed there. It was great entertainment to see them being brought aboard in baskets. The dear souls, they had not seen any European women for a while and before strict discipline was imposed we had to play hide and seek. All was forgiven when they sang for us—something Italians do with flair and beautiful voices!

On the 14th we crossed the equator. There was a dance—no wallflowers there! We reached Aden on the 16th. Being politically naïve we did not quite realize how resentful the Arab population was of the European powers, England especially, after the Suez fiasco. To see the town and to save money, we took the local bus. The mouths of Westerners who saw us fell open in amazement. At the bazaar we stopped at, the police had to come to disperse a crowd of men watching and following us! We should have read the papers more carefully!

On the 17th we entered the Red Sea. I never thought I would actually travel on it. We got off at Suez for a day trip to Cairo and the pyramids. Our little group of four (C., myself, an Irish priest, and a young Swiss man) had a great time speaking French to each other.

First we saw the pyramids in the desert. We went around them on camels! A steep climb inside the big pyramid almost gave me an attack of claustrophobia.

We had tea at the Mena House Hotel with dragoons at the door in fezzes and red uniforms. Then it was on to Cairo and the cemetery, the Ali Mosque, the Tutankhamun Museum, and the bazaar. I bought a cheap pair of slippers. The shopkeeper gave me a little blue scarab (charm), which, he said, guaranteed that I would come back. It was nice, but became not so good later when I discovered that he had given me two slippers of a different size, one small and one large! No wonder I would have to go back!

In Cairo, we had to stop to let a few official cars pass. Nasser, standing in one of them, gave us a great wave that we returned—we were the only four Westerners in the crowd.

On the 22nd, we were on the Mediterranean Sea, and it was not in a good mood. And here I thought it would be like a lake! We reached Brindisi on the 23rd and Venice on the 24th at 2 p.m. What a glorious sight it was. We found a convent for the night. We were alone in a big dormitory and we were so very cold that we slept under piles of blankets from the other beds.

After two days in Venice, it was Milan, Lausanne and Paris. We spent two days in Paris in a small hotel and then on to London where I promptly fell in love with the city, and with Londoners.

Chapter 18

London, England

Jacqueline is in London! We have a room in Earls Court for the moment but are looking for something else. I am so cold that I don't feel like writing … I feel like going to bed. Brrr!

In Venice I got the address of a convent where we could stay. It was an old place, cold as a tomb. I got a cold and I felt that the whole town suffered from it. Imagine that! Us two girls who were dying of the heat just two days earlier! In Venice we couldn't afford gondolas, so we went around the town on foot. St. Marc is the worst monstrosity I have seen—but I liked the Palace of the Doges.

We left Venice by train at 5:30 a.m. It was raining but the sun showed its nose in Switzerland. What a beautiful country it was, so clean with its mountains and its lakes. When we left Switzerland for France, across the Jura I saw some fields under snow—the first snow I have seen since the Himalayas! We looked out at it with round eyes like little girls.

I saw a bit of Burgundy, then Paris. One can't praise Paris enough with its magnificent streets, houses and churches. It was spring weather and we strolled along the Seine. I saw Montmartre, Pigalle, avenue Royale, avenue de l'Opéra, rue Saint-Honoré, faubourg de Rivoli and Avenue des Champs Elysées. What marvels! I will come back.

I had written to a group of lay missionaries for a place to stay in Paris. They found us a room next door to their convent on Saint-Bernardin street. It was a good hotel and cheap too. Only 750 francs for the two of us. The only strange thing about it is that we had to pay for a bath! After booking it with the concierge we found we couldn't afford more than one!

The highlight of my stay was a play at the Théâtre du Vieux Colombier by Luigi Pirandello, *Ce Soir on Improvise* with Carmen and Sacha Pitoëff. We also had a good meal at the "Chèvre du Mas d'Or" on boulevard Saint-Michel.

3 April, 1958   London

Today I have found a job as a secretary for the British Empire and Commonwealth Games organization—imagine that!

I am beginning to know London; and the concerts, the theatre and the ballet. It is enough to make one sick!

After a few days in London, I am suddenly settled in an office that is about a ten-minute walk from Buckingham Palace, and near Bond Street, St. James Palace and Pall Mall. What an important daughter you have! I must say that all these famous names don't mean anything to me or to you. By contrast, all the streets of Paris were familiar as if I had lived there before.

I work for the Empire Games, which are happening in July in Cardiff, Wales. My job will last until the end of August and if all goes well I will go to Scotland and to the Universal Exposition in Brussels. I will see the rest of Europe in a few years when I am rich!

Nothing much has happened here. Next week I will meet K.'s family. They live in Surrey, near London. C. also wants to stay in England longer than we had planned. There is so much to see and do what with the theatre, music and ballet, etc!

I earn seven pounds, ten shillings a week (about 22 dollars) working for the Empire Games. I hope to do better at home. We had to find jobs in London as I told you; it was a question of eating or not. We went to an agent and as luck would have it C. got a position at Dent, the publishing house.

With my typing skills (forty words per minute, never mind if the result was some foreign language yet to be deciphered!), I was sent to the Empire Games office where they collect and seek money for the Games.

I still laugh when I recall how I said that I had come to my job interview by "tub" instead of "tube." It was one of my many near fatal mistakes in English. For the Games, they were very keen to have token Commonwealth (Dominion) people working for them so they hired me. After a few days during which my veritable lack of skills was demonstrated, I was put on files.

In our office in St. James Square, there were two English directors and four girls: two from New Zealand, one from Australia, and me … from Canada. It was great fun. I delivered messages to posh "male clubs" at Buckingham Palace (where the fur-hatted guards didn't even try to stop me, to my great chagrin). We got tickets to plays, greyhound races, vaudeville—and I went to a ball at the Dorchester Hotel with Lord this and Lady that. I bought long black gloves for the occasion. Shades of *La Goulue*! The food for the banquet was mediocre, if not poor, but in that august company what can I say!

At home with C. it was not so good. She was not feeling well, and on the 30th of April was hospitalized. She was in hospital until the 25th of May. I tried to go and see her every day. I also moved to a lovely little bedsitter in Kensington Garden Square while she was away.

I was lucky that my friends at work wanted to see and enjoy London like me, so I went to the Old Vic, Covent Garden, the Royal Festival Hall, the Henley Royal Regatta, and sightseeing with them.

If the hotel in Paris required money for a bath, London also had a surprise for us. On our first night at the hostel in Earls Court we switched on the gas heater—we were so cold. It was wonderful for a while and then … it was gone. We went to complain the next day about a defective heater to be told we had to put money in it! The joys of travelling.

For me, something much more important happened while we

were in London. I went to see K.'s family.

My first visit was very low-key and friendly, "à l'anglaise" I thought. My second was a complete shock. The house was full of people—a real party. All the church VIPs were present. I was not welcomed, so much as appraised. They made no bones about it. I was going to take their golden boy away and lead him straight into the arms of the Pope. To make matters worse, not only was I not of their church, I was not even English but "French", a sure way to hell!

When it became a question of their proud Protestant heritage I knew that as much as K. and I loved each other, this was no family for me. Away from home we might have managed. My family was kind and maybe it would have worked in Canada. K. and I continued to write to each other. I never told him about the reception at his parents' house, but I did not go back to Durban. Amen, as they say.

4 June, 1958   *London*

I must make a decision. I have been offered a job by the YWCA. One is in Vancouver and the other one is in Montréal. Montréal does not seem right for me so I think I will accept Vancouver.

There is very little work for me in Québec. In Vancouver I will earn 328 dollars per month. After a while and with more experience, I might be lucky and find something at home. I don't think that I will stay out West for more than two years.

I have the pleasure to announce that I will be coming home on the Empress of Britain. The ship will leave Liverpool on the 26th of September. I don't know when it will arrive. I am happy that the souvenirs I sent have pleased you. I bought the cameo, maman, in Venice. The tie, papa, is from one of the best shops in London. French perfume is the best for Yolande. I could not go wrong.

When C. was better and back at work, we went to the ballet, concerts, plays, and shows, and did a lot of travelling around London. We also spent four and a half weeks hitchhiking on the continent. First, we went to the Exposition in Brussels, then camping in Paris, Madrid, and Lisbon.

In Lourdes, we put up our tent near a gypsy campsite. It was at the time of their annual pilgrimage. It was very moving to hear them play and sing during the evening candlelight procession. They lifted their instruments during the benediction; it was enough to make you cry.

C. left London on the MV Arosa Sun at the beginning of September. I left a few days later on the Empress of Britain.

Thank you for the 100 dollars. It came just in time. I had to give a deposit in order to hold my reservation on the ship. It is difficult to find a passage in September. All the tourists are going home. I would like to see

Europe thoroughly but that will have to be at a later time.

Tell C. that there were musicians at the entrance of Charing Cross Station after she left. I gave them six pence on behalf of both of us.

Chapter 19

SS Empress of Britain, Canadian Pacific
25,516 tonnes, 1,054 passengers

We were on the St. Lawrence by the 2ⁿᵈ of October. When we reached Pointe-au-Père where the pilots board the ship, I was called to the captain's cabin. To my immense joy, here was one of my uncles, a pilot (though this was not his ship), who had come to greet me with a big box of chocolate and the Québec newspapers. I was crying so much that I could have sunk the ship!

I was on deck all the time taking in this wild and sparsely populated province of mine—only silver steeples and small villages here and there.

When we passed Saint-Laurent (Île d'Orléans), my mother's village, it was dusk. The captain sounded the ship's horn three times and my cousins flicked their car lights on the village quay before leaving to greet me in Québec. What a wonderful sight my hometown is at night!

Of course everyone was waiting on the pier. Another of my uncles (also a pilot) got me through Customs with a wink at the officer. A band was playing, not for me, but for a returning pilgrim group from Lourdes. Nevertheless, it was a glorious and royal welcome back. Just the right finish to five years of vagabondage.

I was home.

— Merci et Thank You —
Denise et Yolande Robitaille
Marguerite et Charles Bujold
Aline Tétreault
Kate Wellburn
Judy Bertram
Lucie Larivière
Alan Schroeder
The staff and volunteers of the Maritime Museum of Victoria
My friends in Australia for 50 years:
Hester Maucham
Peg McCosker
Edna Lawrence
and their families.

Last but not least my husband, Arnie, and our best friends:
our sons Peter, Michael, Jacques,
and their wives, Sandra, Renée, and Heather.

Kobe, 1954

Korea,
25ᵗʰ Canadian Brigade

MV Sibigo

Printed in the United States
by Baker & Taylor Publisher Services